MALCOLM HILLIER

CONTAINER GARDENING

THROUGH THE YEAR

MALCOLM HILLIER

CONTAINER GARDENING

THROUGH THE YEAR

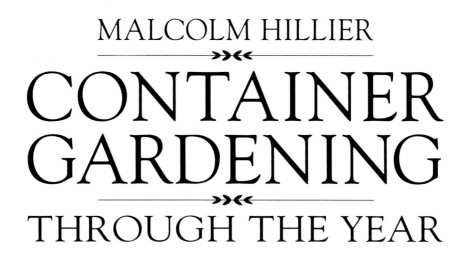

Photography by
MATTHEW WARD

DK PUBLISHING, INC.

www.dk.com

A DK PUBLISHING BOOK

www.dk.com
Project Editor Bella Pringle
Art Editor Louise Bruce
US Editor Ray Rogers
DTP Page Make-up Mark Bracey
Managing Editor Mary-Clare Jerram
Managing Art Editor Amanda Lunn
Production Manager Meryl Silbert

First paperback edition, 1998

First American Edition, 1995
4 6 8 10 9 7 5 3
Published in the United States by Dorling Kindersley
Publishing, Inc., 95 Madison Avenue, New York,
New York 10016
© 1995

Library of Congress Cataloging-in-Publication Data
Hillier, Malcolm
Container gardening through the year. --1st American ed.
p. cm
Includes index.
ISBN 0-7894-3296-X
ISBN 1 56458 869 6 Hardback
1. Container gardening. 2. Container gardening -- Pictorial works
I. Title. II. Title. Container gardening through the year.
SB418.H56 1995   94-26717
635.9'86--dc20   CIP
Text film output by The Right Type, Great Britain.
Reproduced by Colourscan, Singapore.
Printed and bound in Singapore
by Star Standard Industries (Pte.) Ltd.

CONTENTS

FOREWORD

Growing plants in hanging baskets, windowboxes, troughs, pots, and tubs is immensely rewarding and offers great imaginative scope, particularly when gardening in the limited space of a patio, roof terrace, or balcony. Even in large mature gardens, container gardening offers seasonal color and variety and enables you to introduce plants to your garden that you would otherwise not be able to grow in the native soil.

— ❧ *IDEAS FOR CONTAINERS* ❦ —

A surprising number of plants, trees, and shrubs can be grown in pots, and grown well. I hope I can help you by explaining the principles of designing containers for a host of situations. I offer style guidelines for enhancing areas of the garden with imaginatively planted pots, be it a shallow flight of steps, a doorway, a paved patio, a pergola, or a window ledge.

On the following pages, I have put together over 60 container creations for the garden, as well as ideas for inside the house and the conservatory. Focusing on each season in turn, I use a broad selection of plants that are well suited to a huge range of containers and conditions.

FUCHSIA CANOPY

FRAGRANT IRIS

— ❧ *PLANT PARTNERSHIPS* ❦ —

For every featured project, I choose plants that are compatible in growing terms, look beautiful together, and complement the chosen container. While a large part of the book is aimed at the summer months, when it is relatively simple to achieve spectacular results, there are also plenty

of plantings that will give their best display in spring and autumn. I also include planting ideas for indoors and outdoors to help you through the dreary winter months.

BOWL OF PRATIA

— ❧ PRACTICAL ADVICE ❦ —

Each planting is supported by practical advice on how to grow the featured plants successfully. There is detailed information on the number of plants you will need to achieve a rewarding display of color, the most appropriate potting mix, and the plants' water and food requirements. I also recommend the exposure in which they will thrive, whether sunny or shady, sheltered or exposed, and suggest a suitable garden location. I hope you get as much pleasure and inspiration from *Container Gardening Through the Year* as I have had putting together this selection of creative planting ideas.

INTRODUCTION

CONTAINER GARDENING has much to commend it, but perhaps one of its greatest assets is its versatility. By growing plants in pots, you can provide temporary color, where plants can be easily substituted once they are past their peak, as well as permanent interest through the year with perennials, trees, and shrubs.

Raising plants and flowers in pots is especially useful for those with small town gardens or no garden at all. However, it is not simply an idea dreamed up to answer the gardening needs of people with limited space. Its value has been recognized for centuries in garden landscapes the world over, where stately containers filled with a myriad of plants were very popular.

— RAW MATERIALS —

Before detailing the planting ideas I have put together for spring, summer, autumn, and winter, I would like to introduce you to some of the many raw materials available for container gardening, and I would like to help you select the most suitable containers and plants for your needs. First, I will survey the decorative and functional merits of an array of containers, and then outline the advantages and disadvantages of the materials – clay, plastic, copper, or wood – from which they are manufactured. Then I will guide you through the range of plants available to the year-round container gardener.

— BASIC GROUND RULES —

I would also like to share with you a few simple design guidelines that I try to bear in mind when planning my container displays: how to combine a number of pot and plant shapes to achieve pleasing proportions; how to use foliage and flower colors to create different moods; and how to mix different plant textures in displays for maximum interest and variety.

FRAGRANT MIX (*Left*)
In spring, a selection of clay flowerpots filled with hyacinths, grape hyacinths, and narcissus looks especially welcoming on a sunny window ledge.

SUMMER TROUGH (*Right*)
A shady corner of a balcony or patio can be brought to life with this vibrant summer planting of bright orange begonias, pale pink impatiens, and cheerful pansies in shades of pale yellow and white.

CHOOSING THE RIGHT CONTAINER

Selecting the most appropriate container is every bit as important as choosing the plants to grow in them. Materials such as terracotta, fiberglass, stone, and wood all make wonderful containers, and most good garden centers carry an inspirational range of designs. The classic pot shape has gently sloping sides that enable you to remove the plant and its root ball for repotting or planting out. Square pots are useful for plants with extensive root systems since

they hold a greater volume of potting mix for their dimensions than conical pots. When selecting urns and jars that are designed to taper toward the mouth, make sure that the container has a sufficiently wide planting area for your needs. For tall displays, opt for pots with heavy bases to prevent the planting from toppling over. And, if you prefer improvised containers, such as wheelbarrows, remember to provide a drainage hole in the base.

DISTRESSING TERRACOTTA

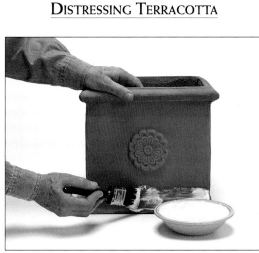

The appearance of most containers improves with age. To speed up the distressing process, paint some live cultured yogurt onto the surface of the pot. Terracotta is very porous and soaks up the moisture quickly; stone pots will take a few days to dry out.

THE RESULT
Place yogurt-painted containers outside in a shady position and, in a month or so, green moss will grow over the surface. Alternatively, place in the sun and the salts in the clay will leach out, forming a white patina.

RUSTIC WOODEN PLANTER

GLAZED CLAY POT

TALL POTS

TERRACOTTA BASKET

INTRODUCTION

SELECTION OF CONTAINERS

An array of pots in different shapes and sizes, made from clay, stone, wood, fiberglass, and metal, gives an idea of the choice of containers available.

CHIMNEY POT

TERRACOTTA STACK

SWAGGED TERRACOTTA POT

LEAD TUB

WOODEN TUB

FIBERGLASS PLANTER

STONE TROUGH

GLAZED CLAY URN

HANGING BASKET

SQUARE WIRE BASKET

COPPER POT

TERRACOTTA WINDOWBOX

TERRACOTTA POT (*Above*)
A time-worn terracotta pot hijacked by lichens and moss has a subtle beauty that does not overpower the delicate planting. Its faded surface blends comfortably with the beige and gray gravel path. With new clay pots, speed up the aging process by following the technique for distressing terracotta outlined on p.10.

— TRADITIONAL TERRACOTTA —

One of the most popular materials for pots has always been terracotta, which means that more pot designs are available in this than in any other medium. Plain or decorative, its rich, earthy color combines beautifully with plants, and it weathers so well that its appearance often improves with age. Terracotta clay is a porous material and quickly soaks up water, so remember to water your plants in terracotta pots frequently to prevent them from drying out.

If you live in a cold area, check that your terracotta containers are frost-resistant: pots imported from Mediterranean countries have a tendency to crack and flake. Unglazed and glazed stoneware is frostproof and more water-retentive. Many terracotta pots are machine-made, but hand-crafted items are always more interesting. If hand-made pots are too expensive for your budget, carefully select mass-produced containers with slight irregularities since these often have greater character and appeal.

— NATURAL WOOD —

Wood is an attractive natural material for tubs, troughs, and windowboxes, and a range of other containers. In damp regions, wood containers have a limited life unless they are made from hardwood. Softwood, however, can be treated with preservative to retard decay, or you can line wooden windowboxes and tubs with plastic to limit rotting caused by watering.

Whisky barrels and half barrels have always been popular plant holders. Now they are made especially for the gardener in a variety of shapes and sizes. Before buying, check that the metal hoops around the barrel are fixed, and that there are no signs of warping.

WOODEN VERSAILLES PLANTER (*Left*)
Tubs coated in wood preservative have a longer life. You can either buy then already treated, or paint them yourself with a clear wood varnish or colored paint, depending on the desired effect.

RECONSTITUTED STONE PLANTER
A reconstituted stone planter soon darkens with age, and its cast moldings can easily be mistaken for expensive sculpted stone.

CONCRETE CHIMNEY POTS
Concrete chimney pots, sprouting with ivy and weeds and arranged on different levels, help to establish this unusual group of containers.

— LEAD AND COPPER —

Plants look particularly attractive in old lead and copper containers, especially when the surfaces of these metals develop a blue-green or gray patina on exposure to the weather. Although metal containers are expensive and very heavy, they last a lifetime. I buy antique containers in traditional designs at auction.

COPPER BOWL
To tarnish a bright copper surface, rub with steel wool and coat in vinegar.

— STONE AND FIBERGLASS —

Stone containers, like lead, are both beautiful and cumbersome. They look magnificent but need to be housed in a permanent site, because moving them about can be a strenuous task. Reconstituted stone or concrete are cheaper alternatives. They can look harsh when brand new, but if treated with cultured yogurt (*see p. 10*), they will soon resemble sculpted stone.

A number of fiberglass containers are designed to simulate natural materials; they are durable, inexpensive, and lightweight.

— IMPROVISED CONTAINERS —

Don't forget those objects that can be adapted to hold plants: chimney pots, wheelbarrows, and sinks can be modified to make containers that lend a special quirky charm to the garden.

CHOOSING THE RIGHT PLANTS

The secret of successful year-round container gardening is to plant a varied selection of trees, shrubs, and flowering perennials in pots to create a foundation of permanent plantings, and then to introduce annuals, biennials, and bulbs that can be easily changed once they are past their peak for temporary seasonal interest.

— SPRING BULBS AND SHRUBS —

Spring is a rich season for the container gardener because a great number of bulbs grow fantastically well in windowboxes, tubs, and troughs. To reap the rewards, plan ahead by planting up bulbs in autumn (*see p.148*). I favor bulbs that smell as good as they look, such as *Narcissus* 'Trevithian'. Early-flowering shrubs like camellias and rhododendrons will also thrive within the confines of containers, as will cherry trees and lilacs, although these will not reach their full height. For extra spring color, plant bulbs around trees and shrubs.

FRESH YELLOW AND PINK SPRING SHOW
Planted up in autumn months, trailing evergreen foliage offers winter interest before the flowering of sweetly scented bulbs in spring. The planting will provide flower color for three or four weeks.

— SUMMER ANNUALS —

By late spring, garden centers are teeming with annuals in a rainbow of colors. Many of them will thrive in the controlled environment of containers, often performing better than in open ground if they are fed and watered at regular intervals. My summer container favorites include scarlet nasturtiums, pink geraniums, and orange begonias, since they provide a splendid show of colorful blooms over many weeks.

FLORIFEROUS SUMMER SELECTION
In summer, many annuals, such as impatiens, petunias, and lobelias, flower simultaneously. With judicious planning and grouping of containers on different levels, you can easily achieve a spectacular show of color and fragrance that spans several months.

— AUTUMN FLOWERS AND BERRIES —

Many of the summer annuals produce a further crop of flowers in autumn. Fuchsias, impatiens, and begonias all put on particularly strong shows of autumn flowers. A few plants, such as Michaelmas daisies, chrysanthemums, and autumn-flowering gentians, come into their own at this time of the year. It is also a good season for berries: pyracanthas and cotoneasters grow well in containers.

AUTUMN DAISIES
(Right)
Osteospermum
flowers get a second
lease on life in autumn.
Mixed with rust-leaved
coleus, they produce a
gloriously autumnal effect.

— WINTER EVERGREENS —

Throughout the year evergreens are invaluable, providing a leafy foil to the more seasonal plants. In the harsh winter months, evergreens such as boxwood and privet are useful. Clipped into simple geometric shapes, they add an architectural beauty to paved patio areas and pathways. In warm winter spells, I often stand pots of cyclamen and azaleas on a table outside my kitchen window, but remember to bring them indoors as soon as the temperature drops. During winter, make container plantings a feature in your home. Hyacinths and narcissus can be encouraged to flower early and, if you are lucky enough to have a garden room or airy conservatory, you could grow winter-flowering jasmine for its fragrance.

WINTER WINDOWBOX
Situated on a sheltered window ledge, winter-flowering heathers and pansies will put on a brave show in areas with mild winters.

AROMATIC KITCHEN HERB GARDEN
Most herbs have Mediterranean origins and favor a bright site. Here, variegated lemon balm sits amid a bed of culinary herbs.

SUN-LOVING NASTURTIUMS AND MARIGOLDS
A wooden trough brimming with scarlet nasturtiums, marigolds, and purple cabbage leaves flourishes in a bright, sunny location. Water the planting regularly to prevent the potting mix from drying out.

— *CHOOSING THE RIGHT SITE* —
When choosing plants for containers, the exposure of the intended site, be it bright, shady, sheltered, or open, should be at the front of your mind. Plants in pots are naturally more exposed to the elements than plants growing in flowerbeds, so the more adept you are at matching the plants' needs to the limitations of the location, the more successful your plantings will be in the long term.

— *BRIGHT SITES: SUN AND SEMISHADE* —
The majority of plants and flowers growing in open ground perform best in bright sites that receive direct sunlight for all or most of the day. When planted up in pots, however, even those varieties that are known sun-worshippers, such as geraniums, grow better in sites where they have respite from the sun. This is because container-grown plants, especially those in hanging baskets, have less soil to retain water; only regular watering will prevent leaves and flowers from scorching in hot, sunny spells.

Areas of a courtyard and north-facing window-sills are often in shade for some, if not all, of the day. Surprisingly, many colorful plants – begonias, hydrangeas, impatiens, azaleas, and rhododendrons – grow well in semishade.

— SHADY POSITIONS —

The most problematic sites are those in deep shade, cast by a tall building or leafy tree. Consider painting garden walls white to reflect light, and plant pots of bright, white-flowered bulbs that are shade-tolerant, such as hyacinths.

— SHELTERED AND EXPOSED SITES —

Protected sites are usually found beside walls or other garden features that act as a windbreak and provide shelter from strong sun and rain. In built-up areas, the temperature is often several degrees warmer than in outlying areas, and so it is possible to grow a range of tender plants very successfully. Exposed sites are more difficult. If there is nothing you can do to create shelter, try planting tough Mediterranean plants in well-drained soil, or select low-growing perennials that will not be battered by wind. Succulents and cacti are also resilient in exposed conditions.

EXPOSED ALPINE TROUGH (*Right*)
In early spring, saxifrages, phlox, and stonecrops — all native to snowy alpine landscapes — grow well in exposed sites.

LOW CAULDRON (*Below*)
Hardy plants, such as scabious and erigeron, grow well in the same container for two or three years. They require little maintenance, and their low-growing habit makes them wind-resistant.

FLOWERING AZALEA FOR SHADE (*Above*)
An azalea, planted in a large tub, produces a profusion of ice pink flowers, bringing instant color to a shady spot. It will flower for a few weeks, and then again in successive years.

PLANTING FOR COLOR

Color is very much a matter of personal taste, but when planning designs for containers, an awareness of the mood color combinations create is important. The color wheel, through which the key principles of color theory are explained, can be used for understanding the effects of color in the garden: red, orange, and yellow evoke a feeling of "warmth," while purple, blue, and green create a "cool" effect.

THE COLOR WHEEL (Right)
Warm colors are those the mind associates with the sun and a sense of well-being; cool colors evoke a soothing, tranquil mood.

HOT RED AND YELLOW COLOR COMBINATION
An effusive mix of bright red, cerise pink, and sunny yellow creates a vibrant mix that sings out against brilliant green foliage.

COOL BLUE AND GREEN COLOR MIX
A harmony of purple-blue hydrangea flowers and green foliage enhances the cool mood of this shady corner of a courtyard.

HARMONY

Harmonious mixes are achieved by combining dark, medium, and light tones of one pigment, or by mixing plants whose colors sit next to one another on the color wheel.

TONES OF RED (*Above*)
Establish harmony by combining a range of dark and light tones of one color. In flower terms, a mix of reds and pinks has this effect.

SUNSET HARMONIES (*Above*)
Flowers and berries in reds, oranges, and yellows – colors that sit next to one another on the color wheel – are truly harmonious.

PINK AND PURPLE HARMONY
Closely harmonious pinkish purple and lilac-blue combine to produce a soft, misty effect that works well with the glazed plum-red container.

CONTRAST

Complementary colors are created by mixing hues that sit diametrically opposite one another on the wheel, such as red and green. Color contrasts are those that do not share a common pigment, such as blue and yellow.

COMPLEMENTARY COLORS (*Above*)
Bright red flowers and green foliage can be optically exhausting. Add gold, purple, or red-tinted foliage to tone down the colors.

PURE CONTRASTS (*Above*)
When working with contrasting colors, use paler color values rather than pure hues, and soften the contrast with green foliage.

CONTRAST TO ORANGE
Vivid orange and deep purple hues create a lively contrast when used in container plantings since these two colors share no pigment in common on the color wheel.

PLANTING FOR PROPORTION AND SHAPE

Plants grow in a variety of different shapes and sizes. To select the most suitable container, and then location, you need to consider a plant's natural habit – upright or trailing, for example – and how tall the plant is going to grow, either in a single season, or until it needs repotting.

When buying shrubs and perennials, always check the dimensions of the plant on the label; annuals are sometimes not labeled for size, so you may have to consult a reference book.

GRAND-SCALE TROUGH
The solid rectangular shape of an antique lead trough is filled with a mound of flowers and foliage that perfectly balances its proportions.

The shape of the pot and planting should look comfortable together. As a visual guideline, plants in containers should not be more than twice the height of the pot, or more than half as wide again as the width.

When grouping a mixed selection of container plantings, their shape, size, and number should be proportionate to the site. Ensure that they all form close-knit groupings, and that they sit at a number of different levels for added interest; one large container can often create a much more pleasing shape than a group of small pots and plants scattered disparately over an area.

— SIX BASIC PLANTING SHAPES —

To achieve pleasing proportions in container displays, it is helpful to bear in mind the six basic design shapes outlined below.

Fan-shaped displays work well in conical pots since the plants grow up and spread out into a bushy fountain of flowers. The second basic shape is a simple rectangle. It can be either vertical, when growing upright plants in a wide pot, or horizontal, if you are using a windowbox or long trough. Both oval- and dome-shaped plantings work well in low-level containers where they can be viewed from above. They should look just as good from the back and the sides as they do from the front. Although rather difficult to achieve, because you can never quite predict the speed or direction of natural plant growth, try altering the center of balance in a display by creating a simple asymmetrical design in a symmetrical container.

1. FAN-SHAPED
Plants and shrubs that splay out into an attractive fan shape work well in terracotta pots that are conical in shape. Select plants that grow to about one-and-a-half times the container height for a balanced display.

2. VERTICAL
To create visual symmetry, try to grow several tall plants together in a single container so that the width of the plants equals the width of the pot. Plant seasonal annuals or foliage around the base.

3. HORIZONTAL
To counteract the long, narrow shape of a windowbox or trough, avoid planting in straight rows, vary the height of the main plants to break up the horizontal thrust, and soften the overall effect with filler plants.

4. OVAL-SHAPED
Oval-shaped containers are often low-level and so look most effective when viewed from above. Plants that are diminutive in stature, or have a characteristic spreading or trailing habit, are the most suitable candidates.

5. DOME-SHAPED
Many plants grow into hummocky shapes, a profile that suits low tubs and cauldrons in exposed sites. Here, trailing foliage helps to break harsh outlines while allowing some of the container's decorative surface to be seen.

6. ASYMMETRICAL
Although perhaps one of the more difficult shapes to achieve, because the proportions of plant material are not equal, asymmetrically planted displays have a movement and instant vitality lacking in more traditional designs.

PLANTING FOR TEXTURE

The ability to work with different flower and leaf textures is as much the key to successful container plantings as an awareness of color and shape. Your choice of textures is governed by where you intend to place your pots. Small feathery leaves and dainty little flowers create delicate plantings whose subtle beauty can be appreciated close up, but to create a display that can be appreciated from a distance, work with bold flowers and large leaf shapes. When working with groups of containers, I often try to choose pots in similar styles to focus attention on the different foliage and flower textures.

BOLD FLOWERS AND DELICATE FOLIAGE (*Above*)
Large Scarborough lilies, set against a background of dainty silver helichrysum and rosettes of succulents, dominate this group.

ESTABLISHING TEXTURAL BALANCE (*Below*)
An equal mix of bold waxy flower and leaf shapes, and smaller feathery flowers and foliage, creates a perfectly balanced selection.

Once you start to look closely at the plants, it becomes clear that flower petals and leaves come in a staggering range of textures. They encompass everything from waxy, smooth, and shiny to matte and prickly, with all the subtle variations in between. When planning displays, try to bear this in mind, and arrange groups of containers at different heights to show off the variety of textures to full advantage.

MIXING FLOWER TEXTURES AND SHAPES (*Above*)
Here, small and large flowerheads in shades of pink create a delicate small-scale planting. Clusters of polygonum pompoms and papery-thin geraniums and phlox mix with velvety petals of cerise petunias.

COMBINING A VARIETY OF LEAF TEXTURES (*Left*)
A variety of leafy textures, shapes, and colors creates an interesting display for a shady site. Waxy dark green begonia leaves combine with splashy variegated houttuynia and trails of creeping Jenny.

GROUPING FLOWERS AND FOLIAGE (*Right*)
A spring group of cylindrical pots demands attention with a series of textures that are strongly at variance with each other. The mossy saxifrages, with their frail-stemmed flowers, stand before an ice pink rhododendron with strong branch shapes and waxy dark green leaves. The frilled green ruff of primrose leaves relates well to the strap-shaped foliage and fluted waxy flowers of calla lilies.

SUITING ARRANGEMENTS TO LOCATIONS

The objective of all container gardeners is to match a single pot or group of containers with the given surroundings. A theme that I cannot stress strongly enough is that the success of your plantings will rest upon your ability to interpret the potential and the limitations of the site from the beginning.

With this in mind, you can choose plants that thrive in the given exposure, select pots made in materials that blend harmoniously with the surroundings, and tailor the shape and scale of your planting so that it sits comfortably within the dimensions of the site. As with most things, common sense and thoughtful planning play a large part. It is all too easy to plant some pots

CLASSICAL FORMALITY (*Below*)
A grand moss-covered urn on a pedestal, filled with vivid pink geraniums, creates an air of formality in this extensive garden.

of plants to stand along a path, only to find that within a season they have grown far too wide, obstructing the passage of passersby.

— ACCESSIBLE SOLUTIONS —

Practical considerations should influence your decisions when planning arrangements for narrow doorways, small windows, and shallow flights of steps. With high-level plantings in particular, make sure that you choose wide window ledges and balconies and that you have secure moorings. Check that plantings can be reached for watering and general maintenance.

— QUICK REMEDIES —

Container plantings can be used as quick, expendable remedies for a number of location problems. For example, containers filled with colorful flowering plants can be dropped in to fill a bare, unsightly hole in a flower border, and tall trees or bushy shrubs planted in pots can create an instant windbreak and protect vulnerable plants growing in flowerbeds.

— INTERPRET THE MOOD —

A specific location may suggest a mood or a theme that can be enhanced by your choice of container plantings. For example, in a garden room you may wish to establish an eastern flavor by planting exotic orchids in clay urns. In a sunny brick courtyard you may be inspired to create a warm, relaxed Mediterranean feel by cramming terracotta pots of red geraniums into every available space, while garden loggias and poolside sites take on a formal classical air when surrounded by pots of boxwood and yew trees.

SPANISH STEPS (*Right*)
Decorative pots of ivy geraniums form an avenue of color up a flight of stone steps. The relaxed welcome they create contrasts with the formal use of similar geraniums in the stone urn (Left).

SPRING

*W*ithout doubt, spring is the most exciting time of the gardening year as we anticipate the warmer weather to come. Dreary cold winter days dissolve into lighter mornings and evenings, and crocuses, daffodils, and cherry blossoms sit against a background of pale blue skies. Soft pastel shades are the predominant hues in nature, and these are echoed in spring plantings. Choose pale creamy yellow primroses and narcissi, and blue-flowering bulbs such as hyacinths and scillas. Their soft shades and perfumes are as fresh as the spring breezes, and nothing later in the year quite matches up to them.

❧❧

PASTEL HUES
Ice blue pots are planted with the pastel flowers of pale pink cherry blossoms, pale blue grape hyacinths, yellow primroses, narcissi, and trailing English ivy. (See p.46 for details.)

CAMELLIA, AZALEA, AND HYACINTHS

☀ SEMISHADE   ⚗ MEDIUM-RICH AND ACIDIC POTTING MIXES   ⚱ MOIST CONDITIONS

JUST AS THE SCENT of the hyacinths begins to perfume the air, the evergreen azalea and camellia shrubs start to put on their spring show. What better way to celebrate these firm favorites than to grow them as a group? I have created a riot of color by combining bright delphinium blue and cardinal red hyacinths, a deep crimson azalea, and a shell pink camellia against a backdrop of dark green leaves. Place the group of terracotta pots on a patio or terrace; they will thrive in the same containers, without replanting, for several years in succession.

HYACINTH
Hyacinthus 'Blue Skies'
*is, in my view, one of the
best blue hyacinths available.*
● 12 bulbs.

AZALEA
Rhododendron
'Vuyk's Scarlet'
*grows very well in pots
and bears brilliant red
flowers in late spring.*
One shrub. ●

HYACINTH ●
Hyacinthus
'Hollyhock' has
double, brilliant
scarlet flowers. After
flowering, plant out
in the garden for the
following year.
12 bulbs.

Terracotta pot; ●
*16in (40cm) deep,
16in (40cm) wide.*

Height
3½ ft
(1.1m)

Terracotta pot ●
*13in (33cm) deep,
13in (33cm) wide.*

◆ GROWING TIPS ◆

Both azaleas and camellias can be planted throughout the year and require acidic soil. Neither shrub tolerates low temperatures, and in cold conditions both are best kept indoors. Plant the large pot of hyacinth bulbs during autumn in a medium-rich potting mix.

CAMELLIA
Camellia japonica 'C.M. Wilson' *has beautiful double shell pink flowers. Always keep just moist.*
• One shrub.

IVY-LEAVED TOADFLAX
Cymbalaria muralis 'Globosa Rosea' *produces small lilac flowers in spring and summer.*
Seven plants. •

ENGLISH IVY
Hedera helix 'Heron's Foot' *has narrow glossy dark green leaves.*
• Four plants.

Toadflax's trailing habit • *makes it well suited to growing in pots; plant in early spring.*

Moss-covered terracotta pot; 32in (80cm) deep, • *18in (45cm) wide.*

BOWL OF PRIMULAS

☀ SUN/SEMISHADE   📗 MEDIUM-RICH POTTING MIX   ⬳ MOIST CONDITIONS

THE PRIMROSE, THE COWSLIP, the polyanthus: many different types of primula are available at garden centers, and many of them flower in spring. The varieties in this bowl planting make ideal companions because they enjoy the same growing conditions and have the same flowering period. Polyanthus, whose cerise flowers form the bulk of this display, are available in a brilliant range of vibrant colors. As a bonus, they also have a sweet scent.

◆ GROWING TIPS ◆

Plant this selection of primulas in spring. Place the bowl in a sunny or semishaded position and deadhead regularly to encourage new flowers. Water occasionally to keep the soil just moist. After flowering, transplant all the plants into the garden to free the pot, but beware of slugs and snails, because they love primulas.

POLYANTHUS
Primula Pacific Series *bears sweet-scented flowers. Buy plants as a mix or as separate colors. Six plants.* ●

COWSLIP
Primula veris has lightly perfumed yellow flowers borne on tall stems.
● *Six plants.*

● POLYANTHUS PRIMROSE
Primula vulgaris 'Eugénie' *is a double purple-blue primrose.* Three plants.

Small terracotta bowl, ●
6in (15cm) deep,
18in (45cm) wide.

Height
24in
(60cm)

FRITILLARIES AND FERNS

☀ SUN/SEMISHADE 🔨 MEDIUM-RICH POTTING MIX ☙ MOIST CONDITIONS

BOTH FERNS AND FRITILLARIES are great favorites of mine. They thrive in the same conditions, so I love to team them up. It is wonderful to see the buds on the tall stems of the snake's-head fritillaries open to reveal nodding bells of exquisite petals with the most beautiful snakeskin markings. The graceful ferns unfurl at just about the same time, to reveal brilliant fronds of spring green foliage.

◆ GROWING TIPS ◆
Plant both fritillary bulbs and ferns in autumn. Grow in a well-drained potting mix, and keep moist though not soggy, especially in cold winter weather. This planting can remain in the pot throughout the year, or you can plant out the fritillary bulbs among rough grass in the garden.

SNAKE'S-HEAD
FRITILLARY
Fritillaria meleagris in a white-flowered form.
Eight bulbs.

SNAKE'S-HEAD FRITILLARY
Fritillaria meleagris has checkered markings with a pink, lilac, purple, or white background. 17 bulbs.

Snake's-head fritillary can be naturalized into rough grass in moist areas.

FERN ●
Polypodium vulgare 'Cornubiense' is an evergreen fern grown for its sculptural form.
Three plants.

Fluted terracotta bowl; 8in (20cm) deep, 14in (35cm) wide.

Height
20in
(50cm)

BASKET OF KALANCHOE

☀ SUN/SEMISHADE   🔱 MEDIUM-RICH POTTING MIX   ⌂ DRY CONDITIONS

FOR THE HOUSE OR CONSERVATORY, the succulent *Kalanchoe pumila* is a magnificent-looking plant that combines beautiful silvery pink foliage with a profusion of violet-pink spring flowers. Another, perhaps better known, kalanchoe, available at garden centers, is *Kalanchoe blossfeldiana*, or flaming Katy. Considerably taller than *K. pumila*, it has many hybrids in a range of colors. I grow *K. pumila* on a bright windowsill during winter then, once the chance of frost has passed, place the display in the garden in semishade; it comes indoors again in autumn. Kalanchoe is suited to growing in a basket since it has a low, spreading habit.

◆ GROWING TIPS ◆

Plant this frost-tender succulent in late summer so that it will be well established by the following spring. Grow in a well-drained potting mix in a site with plenty of bright light, but not direct sun. In winter, keep the plants almost dry and moderately warm. During the spring and summer growing season, water lightly and feed every week. For best results, repot kalanchoe annually in spring.

KALANCHOE
Kalanchoe pumila has tubular violet-pink flowers, ⅓in (1cm) long, that appear in early spring.
Three plants.

Serrate-edged leaves are coated in a white film.

SILVER MOSS
conceals the plastic container in which the kalanchoe is planted.

Wire basket;
11in (28cm) deep,
11in (28cm) wide.

Height
15in
(38cm)

SWEET-PERFUMED IRIS

☼ SUN/SEMISHADE ⚒ MEDIUM-RICH POTTING MIX ⬇ MOIST CONDITIONS

THE IRIS ARE AMONG my favorite flowers. Bearing the name of the Greek goddess of the rainbow, their beautifully formed blooms shimmer in myriad colors from clear yellows through true blues, lilacs, and purples, to deep reds and browns. Many are scented with a perfume reminiscent of Parma violets. These reticulata irises are particularly beautiful and are easily grown from small bulbs. They are short in stature, and all flower in early spring. A sunny garden table is the perfect site to display their blue, purple, and white flowers.

♦ GROWING TIPS ♦

Plant the bulbs in autumn, and place in a sheltered site. Water regularly to prevent the potting mix drying out, but not during severe cold weather. After flowering, feed once a month to ensure good, healthy bulbs the following year.

• After flowering, the leaves double or triple their bloomtime height.

RETICULATA IRIS •
Iris reticulata is a hardy miniature variety of iris. 50 bulbs.

Low terracotta saucer, 4in (10cm) deep, 12in (30cm) wide. •

Height
10in
(25cm)

PANSY AND DAISY HANGING BASKET

☼ SUN/SEMISHADE   🔨 MEDIUM-RICH POTTING MIX   ⚗ MOIST CONDITIONS

FOR THIS DELIGHTFUL hanging basket, I've chosen pink, violet, and purple pansies mixed with white English daisies. Spring pansies are particularly good for this outdoor display of color since they prefer the cool weather at this time of year and, unlike many other spring-flowering plants, they have a sprawling growth that will fill the basket. Double English daisies make ideal companions for the pansies since they are at their best in spring.

◆ GROWING TIPS ◆

Plant the basket in late autumn and, with luck, you will have several pansies flowering during late-winter mild spells. Alternatively, plant in early spring and the display will flower for a month or more. In early summer, the spring pansies and daisies finish flowering, but you can use the ivy again in another planting.

Hanging basket lined with moss, 6in (15cm) deep, 16in (40cm) wide. ●

DOUBLE ENGLISH DAISY
Bellis perennis 'White Carpet', *a large-flowered cultivar, is easily grown to produce a mass of blooms.* Four plants.

PERSIAN BUTTERCUP
Ranunculus asiaticus grows from a tuber and tolerates light frost. Two plants. ●

ENGLISH IVY
Hedera helix 'Harald' *is a compact variety.* Three plants.

PANSY
Viola x *wittrockiana* Universal Series *is available in many colors, and flowers in early spring.* Eight plants. ●

Height 24in (60cm)

WOODLAND WINDOWBOX

☀ SUN/SEMISHADE   🔱 MEDIUM-RICH POTTING MIX   🗮 MOIST CONDITIONS

I LIKE TO GROW spring plantings with a foundation of evergreen foliage to give winter interest before the arrival of the flowers. Here, the periwinkles and English ivies have variegated leaves and the primulas display attractive leaf rosettes. During late winter, the narcissi start to push through the soil, and by mid-spring the windowbox is brimming with sky blue, pink, and pale yellow flowers. What's more, the display will give you pleasure for as long as three to four weeks.

◆ GROWING TIPS ◆

Plant this windowbox in autumn. If you grow greater periwinkle in your garden, carefully lift small clumps and transplant them into the windowbox. Plant the small narcissus bulbs 2in (5cm) deep and close together in small groups, between the primulas and periwinkles. Deadhead flowers regularly and trim fading foliage.

NARCISSUS
Narcissus triandrus 'April Tears.' 25 bulbs. ●

● **DRUMSTICK PRIMULA**
Primula denticulata has globes of pink flowers. Three plants.

GREATER PERIWINKLE
Vinca major 'Variegata'. ● Three plants.

ENGLISH IVY
Hedera helix 'Kolibri' has silver-splashed green leaves. ● Four plants.

Terracotta windowbox; 10in (24cm) deep, ● *22in (55cm) long.*

Height 24in (60cm)

ORCHID CACTUS AND CLIVIA

☼ BRIGHT SHADE 🖌 MEDIUM-RICH POTTING MIX ⚱ DRY CONDITIONS

ORCHID CACTUS AND CLIVIA are among a host of tender plants that will not survive outside in cold weather, but they can tolerate low temperatures if they are kept in a garden room or conservatory. Indeed, I have found that many tropical plants will thrive in these conditions if they are kept dry in colder spells until early spring, when they begin to grow again. A bright, but not sunny, window ledge that receives early morning or late afternoon sun is best, and in summer they can stand outside in a sheltered site.

◆ GROWING TIPS ◆

Plant both pots when indoor light levels are naturally good. Feed once a month with liquid high-phosphorus fertilizer to encourage flowering.

Grow in the same pot for several years; clivias flower best if their roots are confined. •

ORCHID CACTUS •
Nopalxochia phyllanthoides has pink flowers held on glossy green stems. One plant.

CLIVIA •
Clivia miniata bears several orange flowers on each stem in spring.
Two plants.

• *Stakes support flowering stems and encourage upright growth.*

Dark blue glazed pot; 10in (25cm) deep, 12in (30cm) wide. •

Height
34in
(85cm)

EXOTIC ORCHIDS

☀ BRIGHT SHADE 🖌 ORCHID POTTING MIX ⚱ MOIST CONDITIONS

HERE ARE TWO ORCHIDS that are relatively simple to grow indoors: one with delicate sprays of tiny flowers, and the other with larger, beautifully marked flowers in subdued purples and pinks – not the type that springs to the mind's eye when the name "orchid" is mentioned, but still beautiful. Once their flowers have finished (and they last a long time), the strap-shaped evergreen leaves remain an attractive feature of these plants. During the summer months, keep both orchids outside in a shady position in the garden.

◆ GROWING TIPS ◆
Plant at any time of year, using a prepared orchid potting mix or your own mix made from two parts fine, shredded bark to one part sphagnum moss. Water regularly and feed with a weak solution of fertilizer, little and often throughout the summer.

SLIPPER ORCHID
Paphiopedilum 'King Arthur'. Repot annually for best results.
● Two plants.

MOTH ORCHID
Phalaenopsis equestris has delicate pink flowers. Repot every three years.
One plant. ●

Glossy dark green leaves. ●

Small wire basket, 10in (25cm) deep, 10in (25cm) wide. ●

● *Wire basket, 14in (35cm) deep, 14in (35cm) wide.*

Orchid potting mix, ● though well drained, should not be allowed to dry out completely.

● *Sphagnum moss hides the plastic lining perforated with drainage holes.*

Height
18in
(45cm)

SHELTERED COURTYARDS

SPACE SAVERS (*Left*)
In autumn, a trellis framework on a sheltered wall is imaginatively hung with Boston and maidenhair ferns, and vivid scarlet cyclamen.

TABLETOP FEATURE (*Right*)
A garden table in a city courtyard is set with miniature rhododendrons, callas, primulas, and saxifrages. (See pp. 40-41 for details.)

SHADY RETREAT (*Below Left*)
Bright cerise-colored fuchsias and variegated felicia foliage grow particularly well in a striped tub in a shady site until the first frosts.

ENCHANTED GARDEN (*Below Right*)
Throughout summer, a magical corner is home to a statue that peers out from behind pots of hebe, hydrangea, and impatiens.

COMPOSITION IN PINK

☼ SEMISHADE ⚒ MEDIUM-RICH, ACIDIC, AND ALKALINE POTTING MIXES ⚯ MOIST CONDITIONS

B Y GROUPING TOGETHER different plants in their own terracotta pots, you can satisfy each plant's needs while bringing together a diverse and attractive mix of colors and shapes that you would not normally see growing side by side. The miniature rhododendron prefers well-drained acidic soil, and the saxifrages require a gritty alkaline potting mix. Both will survive mild winters in a sheltered courtyard. The pink callas and primroses, on the other hand, enjoy a medium-rich potting mix and are frost tender; keep them indoors over winter for protection. In spring, all these relatively small-growing plants are at their best and make a perfect group for a low garden table.

MOSSY SAXIFRAGE •
Saxifraga 'Appleblossom'
produces masses of pink flowers;
Saxifraga 'Four Winds'
(far right) has cerise flowers.
One plant per pot.

Dense hummock of •
deeply divided leaves has
a mosslike appearance.

◆ GROWING TIPS ◆

Plant all the pots in autumn in the appropriate potting mix. *Primula obconica* is perennial, but it performs best in pots if grown for one season only. Bring the callas and primroses indoors during winter for protection.

MINIATURE RHODODENDRON
*Rhododendron mackii is hardy
and bears ice pink flowers set
off by dark evergreen foliage.*
• One shrub.

• **CALLA**
*Zantedeschia
rehmannii bears
flowers for up to
three months.*
Three plants.

• *Tapering mid-
green leaves are
sometimes flecked
with silvery white
and are generally
pest-free.*

*Large terracotta pot;
5in (12.5cm) deep,*
• *5in (12.5cm) wide.*

• **GERMAN
PRIMROSE**
*Primula obconica
produces pink, red, or
white flower clusters.
The leaves can cause
skin allergies, so take
care.* One plant.

Small terracotta pot; •
*4in (10cm) deep,
4in (10cm) wide.*

Height
20in
(50cm)

GRAPE HYACINTHS AND NARCISSI

☼ BRIGHT SHADE   ⌗ MEDIUM-RICH POTTING MIX   ⬗ MOIST CONDITIONS

Bright yellow narcissi and blue grape hyacinths possess the colors and fragrances that epitomize spring. They both grow easily from bulbs, and I like to plant them as a pair in terracotta containers close to the house. For perfume, they are winners. The hyacinths have a buttery scent, while the 'Trevithian' narcissi have an almost tropical fragrance, which is even stronger than that of the jonquil, their parent. When these gems are in full flower, I position them next to a garden seat so that on warm spring days I can inhale their lovely sweet perfume.

◆ GROWING TIPS ◆

Plant both the narcissus and grape hyacinth bulbs in autumn to flower the following spring. Place the pots in a bright site. After flowering, dig up the bulbs and plant them out in the garden, where they will soon naturalize.

NARCISSUS •
*Narcissus 'Trevithian'
has fragrant, clear sunny
yellow flowers. 50 bulbs.*

GRAPE HYACINTH
*Muscari armeniacum
'Blue Spike' has a short
stem, double flowers, and a
buttery scent. 50 bulbs.* •

• *Terracotta pot,
12in (30cm) deep,
12in (30cm) wide,
painted with yogurt
to foster moss.*

• *Terracotta basin,
12in (30cm) deep,
34in (85cm) wide.*

Height
34in
(85cm)

FRAGRANT LILAC TREE

☀ SUN   🖌 MEDIUM-RICH POTTING MIX   ✧ DRY CONDITIONS

ALONG WITH SWEET PEAS, lilacs produce one of the greatest flower perfumes, and this miniature lilac is no exception. It has that true lilac fragrance, with a hint of wisteria and violet in its mix. Each year, in spring, it produces a profusion of long-lasting lavender-pink spires. 'Palibin' is ideal for growing in a pot, since it will not exceed a height of 5ft (1.5m) – a good choice for small-scale gardens that cannot accommodate the larger types of lilacs available.

◆ GROWING TIPS ◆

Plant the miniature lilac tree in autumn. With good drainage and an occasional summer feeding, this low-growing species should be happy in its terracotta pot for a few years. Deadhead and prune after flowering. Plant toadflax in early spring.

• Cut out weak
shoots in winter
to achieve a more
compact plant.

MINIATURE LILAC •
Syringa meyeri 'Palibin'
is hardy and produces
fragrant lilac-pink flowers
in late spring and during
early summer. One tree.

IVY-LEAVED TOADFLAX •
Cymbalaria muralis 'Globosa
Rosea' has pale pink flowers
and bright green kidney-shaped
leaves. It will thrive for several
years within the confines of
a container. Nine plants.

• Terracotta pot
12in (30cm) deep,
18in (45cm) wide.

Height
34in
(85cm)

DECORATIVE DOORWAYS

FRAGRANT VERBENA JAR *(Left)*
Verbena 'Sissinghurst' and trailing ivy-leaved Pelargonium 'Rouletta' introduce color and fragrance to a sunny doorway.

BEGONIA BASKET *(Right)*
A hanging basket of red, pink, and white begonias brings a show of color to a shady entrance from summer until the first frosts.

SPRING WELCOME *(Below Left)*
Open the door to a fresh bulb planting of purple-striped Crocus 'Pickwick' and deep blue scilla. (See p.47 for details.)

COTTAGE DOORWAY *(Below Right)*
Pots of impatiens in shades of pink look very much at home sitting alongside a mellow red brick entrance porch.

BLOSSOMING CHERRIES

☀ SUN   🖌 MEDIUM-RICH POTTING MIX   ⥺ MOIST CONDITIONS

WHAT COULD BE more appropriate for a spring planting than a mix of miniature cherry trees in blossom, sweet-scented yellow primroses, and pale blue grape hyacinths? Contrary to popular belief, most trees can be planted in pots and, if they are potted on into increasingly larger containers, they will grow to a good size, though not as large as trees grown in open ground. A sunny wall against the house is the most suitable location; if you opt for a more exposed site, remember to stake the trees. (*See p.150 for details.*)

◆ GROWING TIPS ◆

Plant the cherry trees, grape hyacinth bulbs, and primrose plants in early autumn. After flowering, cut back the shoots of the cherry trees close to the top of each tree trunk. Remove the primroses and grape hyacinths and plant them out in the garden. In their place, plant summer-flowering annuals or English ivy, which will last throughout the year.

CHERRY •
Prunus triloba bears masses of double, pale pink blossoms on branches during midspring.
One tree per pot.

• *Prunus triloba has a dense, twiggy habit. It can grow to a height and spread of 10ft (3m).*

GRAPE HYACINTH •
Muscari azureum carries long-lasting pale blue flowers.
25 bulbs per pot.

• **PRIMROSE**
Primula vulgaris. After flowering, plant out this clump-forming perennial in the garden where it will naturalize.
Six plants per pot.

Height
4ft 7in
(1.4m)

• *Lime-washed terracotta pot; 15in (38cm) deep, 18in (45cm) wide.*

HARBINGERS OF SPRING

☀ SUN   ⚒ MEDIUM-RICH POTTING MIX   ⚘ MOIST CONDITIONS

THE EARLIEST SPRING-FLOWERING BULBS are always a cheering sight, announcing that winter is drawing to a close. Often, there can be more bad weather to come, but somehow, once these bulbs start to flower, the promise of warmer days is real. It is always worth planting spring bulbs such as crocus and scilla *en masse*. What's more, if you buy them in bulk, they are not too expensive. Even though crocuses and scillas are remarkably hardy plants, these low plantings grow best in a sheltered spot. The scillas flower continuously for almost a month, but crocus flowers last only a few weeks.

◆ GROWING TIPS ◆

In autumn, plant the pans so that each bulb is close to the next. The pans must have good-sized drainage holes to prevent the bulbs from becoming waterlogged and rotting. Place the pans in a sheltered site through the winter, and keep moist. After flowering, plant the bulbs out into the garden. 'Pickwick' crocuses naturalize well in rough grass.

CROCUS
Crocus 'Pickwick'. Each bulb produces two or three flowers that last for about two weeks.
50 bulbs per pan. ●

SCILLA
Scilla siberica 'Spring Beauty'. These miniatures carry intense blue flowers throughout early spring.
50 bulbs per pan. ●

● *Shallow stone pan; 4in (10cm) deep, 20in (50cm) wide.*

Height
10in
(25cm)

SPRING ALPINE TROUGH

☀ SUN 🍴 MEDIUM-RICH POTTING MIX WITH GRAVEL ⚒ DRY CONDITIONS

W HEN WINTER SNOWS on mountain slopes are melted by the warm sun,
many alpine plants growing in rocky crevices burst into flower.
Capture the essence of a rocky alpine landscape by planting a trough with
alpine species. If you don't have a genuine stone trough, you can
buy one that is made from reconstituted stone or use an
old porcelain sink. Saxifrages, phlox, and stonecrops
with their sprays of pink flowers all grow well in
simulated alpine conditions and look their best
in late spring. Place the weathered stone
trough on a paved area in an open site,
where it can be seen to full advantage.

HENS AND CHICKS
Sempervivum 'Commander
Hay' *bears purplish rosettes*
of leaves. In summer,
the center produces
a stem of flowers.
Three plants. ●

◆ GROWING TIPS ◆

Good drainage is essential when growing alpines. Make sure that your trough has a drainage hole situated at its lowest point. Cover this with bits of broken pots or pieces of screening. Using an equal mixture of medium-rich potting mix and fine-grain gravel, plant the trough in autumn or early spring, in a bright sunny situation. Once the saxifrages have finished flowering, replace them with other plants, such as miniature poppies and erodiums, for continued interest.

Fine-grain gravel is added to medium-rich potting mix to ● *aid drainage.*

STONECROP
Sedum spathulifolium 'Purpureum' is an evergreen species with fleshy ● *purple leaves. Three plants.*

SAXIFRAGE
Saxifraga 'Southside Seedling' grows well in rocky crevices. ● *Three plants.*

● **PHLOX**
Phlox adsurgens 'Wagon Wheel' is a perennial species that flowers for two months during late spring and summer. One plant.

● *Weathered stone trough; 8in (20cm) deep, 28in (70cm) long.*

Height
22in
(55cm)

AZALEAS AND AJUGA

✳ SEMISHADE　🔥 ACIDIC POTTING MIX　🝳 MOIST CONDITIONS

A ZALEAS OFFER AN ENORMOUS RANGE of flower colors, from clear red, lilac, and purple, to brilliant orange, as well as a gamut of pastel shades. What is more, many of the deciduous varieties, including this glorious orange 'Gloria Mundi', have a rich spicy scent, and colorful red autumn foliage provides a second season of interest. In striking contrast, the delicate violet-flowered ajugas weave an evergreen carpet around the base of the fiery azaleas. Place the pots in a sheltered position where they will be well protected from wind and cold.

◆ GROWING TIPS ◆

Azaleas should be planted in early spring to give the plants enough time to become established before the onset of colder winter weather. Unlike some members of the large rhododendron genus, they tolerate sunshine. Water regularly, and feed occasionally during the summer.

AZALEA
Rhododendron 'Gloria Mundi' *grows to a height of 5ft (1.5m) and has scented orange flowers.*
● One shrub per pot.

Shallow roots make azaleas easy to transplant, but they should never be allowed to dry out. ●

● *Square, well-worn terracotta pot; 16in (40cm) deep, 16in (40cm) wide.*

AJUGA
Ajuga reptans 'Atropurpurea'. *In the past its purple flowers and leaves were used to treat jaundice.* Six plants per pot.

Height
3ft
(1m)

Tulip Blaze

✲ SUN/SHADE · MEDIUM-RICH POTTING MIX · MOIST CONDITIONS

FEW PLANTINGS ARE MORE striking than a large terracotta pot brimming with richly scented scarlet tulips. With very little effort on your part, they make a colorful statement, and their perfume carries well. At the beginning of spring their petals are closed tight, but they soon begin to open out, revealing their dark centers. Most spring-flowering bulbs are hardy, but they prefer bright situations. I have planted these tulips on my terrace, where they get plenty of light but not much sunshine. When I look out of my kitchen window, the splash of color is a cheering sight on even the grayest of days.

Tulips, originally from Turkey, have been popular in Europe for the last 400 years.

TULIP *Tulipa 'De Wet' has bright red flowers with a rich scent. Deadhead blooms when the first petals fall.* 50 bulbs.

Planting bulbs in autumn gives tulips time to develop a strong root system before the cold weather sets in.

Swag-motif terracotta pot; 28in (70cm) deep, 22in (55cm) wide.

◆ Growing Tips ◆

Plant tulip bulbs in autumn. If the pot is very large, fill the base with broken-up pieces of polystyrene. Then fill the container with potting mix and firm the soil to within just 8in (20cm) of the rim. Arrange a layer of bulbs on the soil surface, then add potting mix, firming as you go, until the pot is filled to within 2in (5cm) of its rim. Keep the soil moist during winter, and support the stems with stakes as they grow. After flowering, deadhead them and transplant the bulbs into the garden.

Height 3ft (1m)

SUMMER

Summer has arrived and, as the days lengthen, there is an outpouring of color and scent. The garden is awash with flowering plants and shrubs, and the early morning air shimmers with the promise of warmth. This is the time of year for outdoor living, and the pleasure of idling away the hours sitting on the patio talking and eating is even greater when you are surrounded by glorious pots of fragrant plants. Even if you don't have a garden, you can still capture the heady scents of summer by growing a mixture of flowers and foliage in a windowbox.

❧

SUNNY WINDOWBOX
Creamy yellow osteospermum flowers grow up toward the sunlight, while trails of soft pink ivy geranium flowers, English ivy, and variegated tradescantia foliage spill over the edges of this white wooden windowbox. (See p.75 for details.)

SUMMER GOLDS

☀ SUN/SEMISHADE   🖌 MEDIUM-RICH POTTING MIX   ⚚ MOIST CONDITIONS

A SUNNY MIX OF YELLOW, cream, and silver flowers and foliage spills out to create this sparkling windowbox display. Golden marigolds and lemon yellow petunias with their bold flowers form the focus of the arrangement, while feathery sedum and spiky lutea foliage add textural interest. A pair of these windowboxes sits on the two sunny window ledges outside my dining room, echoing the warm yellow and cream color theme within. The windowboxes continue to look fantastic through- out the summer and autumn.

AFRICAN MARIGOLD •
*Tagetes erecta is a fast-
growing annual. For
optimum flowering
deadhead regularly.*
Three plants.

*Fluted terracotta
windowbox;
8in (20cm) deep,
31in (78cm) long.* •

Height
20in
(50cm)

PETUNIA
*Petunia x hybrida has small
lemon yellow flowers that are
less easily damaged by rain
than those of grandiflora
hybrids.* Four plants. •

SEDUM
*Sedum lineare does
well in summer but
is not hardy enough
to survive frost.*
Three plants. •

◆ **GROWING TIPS** ◆
Plant the terracotta windowbox in
spring when the chance of frost has
passed. Deadhead marigolds and
petunias frequently to encourage a
succession of flowers throughout the
summer months. Cut back petunia
stems when they start to get leggy
and they will soon produce
new flowering shoots. Be on
the look out for aphids: they
tend to attack young plants.

LUTEA
*Monopsis lutea has a
trailing habit, which
softens the edges of
the windowbox.*
• Three plants.

A PROFUSION OF PINKS

☼ SUN/SEMISHADE   ▮ MEDIUM-RICH POTTING MIX   ⬰ MOIST CONDITIONS

SHADES OF PINK and a touch of bright white are combined to create this delicate color mix. Vivid pink ivy-leaved geraniums form the centerpiece of the hanging basket, while soft, feathery upright plumes of pale pink diascia play a strong supporting role. Fronds of purple-pink verbena, tuffets of pink lobelia, and delicate white reinwardtia flowers are threaded through the edges and base of the basket to create a frothy, natural arrangement.

• GROWING TIPS •

Plant the basket in early summer. Position geraniums, diascia, and verbena in the center of the basket, and the lobelia and reinwardtia at the sides. (*See p.149.*) Feed weekly with a high-phosphorus fertilizer. Water and deadhead regularly, and cut back straggly verbena stems.

PHLOX
Phlox drummondii Beauty Series *produces clusters of star-shaped flowers from summer to early autumn.*
• Two plants.

DIASCIA •
Diascia vigilis also makes an attractive border plant.
Two plants.

VERBENA
Verbena hybrids. As with many plants, the paler colors, especially pinks and whites, have the strongest fragrance.
Two plants. •

IVY-LEAVED
GERANIUM
Pelargonium peltatum 'Madame Crousse' *is a good choice for a hanging basket since it produces trailing stems up to 3ft (1m) long.*
Three plants.

REINWARDTIA •
Reinwardtia trigyna is frost tender.
Three plants.

• *Wire basket; 6in (15cm) deep, 16in (40cm) wide.*

Height
32in
(80cm)

LOBELIA •
Lobelia pendula 'Lilac Cascade'.
Three plants.

SHIMMERING SILVER AND VIOLET

☀ SUN/SEMISHADE   🛠 MEDIUM-RICH POTTING MIX   🧺 MOIST CONDITIONS

VIOLETS AND PANSIES are ideal candidates for hanging baskets because they grow rapidly to form a mound of green leaves surmounted by a continuous show of flowers. Here, lilac-colored horned violets are mixed with soft yellow and white pansies to create a subtle color note. The effect is enhanced by a cascade of trailing plectranthus foliage and silver-gray helichrysum. Hang the basket in a bright position, but out of direct sunlight, and it will perform well through the summer.

• GROWING TIPS •

Plant the hanging basket after the chance of frost has passed. Deadhead the pansies regularly and cut back long straggly stems. Feed the plants weekly; water frequently, especially in dry weather. Trim helichrysum foliage to keep in bounds.

• PANSY
Viola x wittrockiana 'Antique Shades' *has small lemon yellow, pink, lavender, or pale peach flowers.* Three plants.

HORNED VIOLET •
Viola cornuta 'Lilacina' *produces a mass of fragrant flowers over several months.* Two plants.

PANSY •
Viola x wittrockiana 'Paper White' *has exquisite white flowers with a bright yellow center.* Two plants.

PLECTRANTHUS •
Plectranthus coleoides 'Variegatus' *is a frost-tender perennial with aromatic sage-scented leaves.* Three plants.

• HELICHRYSUM
Helichrysum petiolare. A useful trailing plant for hanging baskets. Three plants.

Height
28in
(70cm)

Wire basket, 6in (15cm) deep,
16in (40cm) wide.

FLOWER-FILLED BORDERS

ON A PEDESTAL (*Left*)
A stone urn sits on a pedestal above a boxwood-edged flowerbed. Here, magenta geraniums, trailing white lobelia, and silver helichrysum produce a shimmering effect against a backdrop of clipped yew hedges.

SILVER AND BLUE HUES (*Right*)
In summer, indigo blue larkspur, filigrees of senecio, and trails of helichrysum foliage will grow prolifically in terracotta pots. This movable feast brings interest to a flower-free space in a border. (See p.60 for details.)

COLORFUL FILLERS (*Below*)
A narrow border in front of a clematis-covered wall is treated to a brilliant planting of vivid scarlet dahlias and a jumble of lilac campanula flowers in beautifully weathered terracotta pots. (See pp.62-63 for details.)

SEA OF BLUE LARKSPUR

✺ SUN　🖌 MEDIUM-RICH POTTING MIX　🖘 MOIST CONDITIONS

TRUE BLUE FLOWERS such as larkspur, plumbago, hydrangeas, and gentians are not commonplace, but they can play a very special part in container gardening. Here, vivid blue larkspur is set against the silver plumes of *Senecio maritima* 'Silver Dust' and the delicate, trailing leaves of *Helichrysum petiolare*. This silver mix of foliage seems to intensify the rich blue hue of the larkspur flowers. Stand the terracotta pot in the middle of a herbaceous border or use it to add extra interest to a paved area.

◆ **GROWING TIPS** ◆
In cold regions where late frosts are likely, delay planting the pot until midspring because helichrysum and senecio cannot tolerate frost. Larkspur is hardy but not long-lasting.

LARKSPUR
Delphinium consolida 'Blue Cloud' *is a hardy dwarf* ● *variety.* Four plants.

SENECIO ●
Senecio maritima 'Silver Dust' *has yellow flowers. Remove them to encourage healthy, bushy foliage.* Three plants.

Terracotta pot, ●
16in (40cm) deep, 19in (48cm) wide.

● HELICHRYSUM
Helichrysum petiolare has gray-felted leaves and is grown as an annual. Three plants.

Height
34in
(85cm)

PINK MIST

☼ SUN/SEMISHADE ⚱ MEDIUM-RICH POTTING MIX ⚑ MOIST CONDITIONS

WHEN PLANNING SUMMER COLOR, don't rely just on annuals: take a longer-term view. There are a number of beautiful perennials that produce a wealth of flowers over the summer months. This planting of scabious and erigeron bears rich pink flowers from early summer to autumn, and they will continue to thrive in the same container for two or three years, needing very little maintenance. The cauldronlike shape of the large terracotta pot is ideally suited to the low-growing habit of scabious and erigeron plants. I've used trails of English ivy to spill over and soften the container's edges. Place on the edge of a herbaceous border.

◆ **GROWING TIPS** ◆

Plant these hardy species in early spring. To prevent the fast-growing ivies from taking over the entire pot in the second season, thin them out and fill in the holes with potting mix.

Allow several of the scabious flowers to go to seed. Seedheads make an attractive addition to the display.

SCABIOUS
Scabiosa caucasica 'Pink Mist' bears rich pink flowers. Three plants.

ERIGERON
Erigeron 'Charity' has a low-growing, spreading habit. Three plants.

ENGLISH IVY
Hedera helix 'Gavotte' carries small, elongated, dark green leaves. Four plants.

Terracotta cauldron, 15in (38cm) deep, 10in (25cm) wide.

Height
30in
(75cm)

REGAL MIX

☀ SUN 🧑 MEDIUM-RICH POTTING MIX ⚱ MOIST CONDITIONS

LOW-GROWING DAHLIAS have great appeal: they are available in a staggering range of colors; they flower later than many other summer plants; and, unlike the giant-flowered varieties, they don't require staking. Here, dahlias are teamed up with *Campanula poscharskyana*, a long-lived hardy perennial that seeds itself freely and enjoys growing in cracks and crevices in old stone walls and paths. Luckily, this campanula also thrives in pots, and it produces several flushes of flowers from early summer until the first frosts in autumn.

CAMPANULA ●
Campanula poscharskyana
spreads quickly. Its bell-shaped
violet flowers soon pour over
the sides of the container.
Four plants per pot.

◆ GROWING TIPS ◆

Plant dahlias and campanula in pots in early summer. To keep dahlias bushy, take out tall growing tips and, once in bloom, deadhead regularly to reward yourself with a continual show of red flowers. After the first flush of campanula flowers, trim back the plants to encourage more flowering stems. Watch for spider mites and aphids on the dahlias.

Terracotta pot, ●
17in (43cm) deep,
20in (50cm) wide.

Height
34in
(85cm)

DAHLIA
Dahlia 'Sunny Red' is
rewarding for both its intense
color and prolific flowering.
Three plants per pot. ●

Dahlias make excellent cut
flowers and bloom continuously
throughout summer.

Campanula also
grows well between
the stones and bricks
in old walls.

● *Terracotta pots*
kept outdoors all year
must be frostproof or
they will crack and flake.

POOLSIDE PLANTINGS

DAPPLED SHADE *(Left)*
A Chinese glazed hexagonal pot, spilling over with lilac-colored lobelia, blue phacelia, and silver helichrysum, sits beside a terracotta pan of pratia displaying a delicate mound of blue star-shaped flowers. On the edge of a small pool overgrown with duckweed, these container plantings make a tranquil focal point for a shady retreat. (See p.66 for details.)

PURPLE HAZE *(Right)*
A selection of pots and urns, brimming with rich purple campanula, deep red dianthus, and pink geraniums, is arranged on a number of different levels to add interest to this informal paved pool area. The pool itself is filled with tall-growing, leafy iris plants.

SIMPLE BEAUTY *(Above)*
White fibrous-rooted begonias in a square wooden trough enjoy the humidity of a watery location. Set against a backdrop of large water lily leaves, this planting looks all the better for its simplicity. (See pp.68-69 for details.)

SENSORY DELIGHT *(Right)*
At the edge of the pool, an old lead trough overflowing with bright pink geraniums and scented verbena combines with the sound of splashing water from an attractive shell-shaped fountain, to delight the senses.

COOL BLUES

☼ SEMISHADE   🌿 MEDIUM-RICH POTTING MIX   ⚘ MOIST CONDITIONS

PHACELIA WITH ITS DELICATE azure blue flowers, a froth of lilac lobelia, and trails of silver-gray helichrysum create a distinctly cool combination. Phacelia is an unusual choice but well worth remembering when you consider the lack of true blue-colored flowers available. Lobelia, on the other hand, is a very popular trailing plant because it grows quickly, filling out the display. Available in clear, pale, and deep blues, purples, lilacs, and pinks, lobelia produces a mass of flowers for months on end. To show off this planting to best advantage, place it in a shady poolside location.

◆ GROWING TIPS ◆

Plant the pot in early summer. Water regularly to keep the potting mix moist, and feed at least once a week. Phacelia can be cut back after its first flowering to encourage a second crop of flowers. Trim the helichrysum stems periodically to prevent the plants from becoming too long and straggly.

LOBELIA
Lobelia erinus spreads rapidly and blooms until the first frosts.
● Five plants.

PHACELIA
Phacelia campanularia carries deep blue flowers that are attractive to bees from early to late summer.
Four plants.

Phacelia leaves are fragrant when crushed.

HELICHRYSUM
Helichrysum petiolare is an evergreen shrub. Remove creamy yellow flowers to encourage healthy, bushy foliage.
Four plants.

Height
24in
(60cm)

● *Hexagonal glazed pot; 20in (50cm) deep, 24in (60cm) wide.*

CORAL AND JADE

☼ BRIGHT SHADE   🖌 MEDIUM-RICH POTTING MIX   🗸 MOIST CONDITIONS

OFTEN THE SIMPLEST of plantings can give the greatest joy. Here impatiens – a celebrated container plant – is paired with miniature bamboo grass to great effect in terms of color and texture. This New Guinea hybrid, with its coral-colored flowers, has only recently become available at garden centers, and is distinguished from other types by the crystalline sheen on its petals and larger leaf size. Other colors range from rich cyclamen pink and bright orange to subtle shades of lilac and salmon pink. Both impatiens and bamboo enjoy a bright position and look at home near a water garden.

◆ GROWING TIPS ◆

Plant the pot after the chance of frost has passed because both New Guinea hybrids and miniature bamboo grasses are frost tender. Keep the plants well watered, and feed at least twice monthly so that the impatiens flower continuously throughout the summer months. To avoid rot, remove dead flowerheads that drop into the planting.

BAMBOO GRASS
Pogonatherum paniceum has pink leaf tips that work well with the coral pink impatiens.
● Three plants.

IMPATIENS
Impatiens New Guinea hybrid *is a robust plant with glistening coral-colored flowers.* Three plants. ●

Height
20in
(50cm)

Green glazed pot; ●
12in (30cm) deep, 20in (50cm) wide.

SHADE-LOVING COMPANIONS

☀ BRIGHT SHADE 🍴 MEDIUM-RICH POTTING MIX ⚱ MOIST CONDITIONS

FEW FLOWERING PLANTS actually enjoy growing in shade, but these are two that will flourish. Variegated wandering Jew is usually grown indoors, but it will do terrifically well outside in containers and hanging baskets if it is given a warm, sheltered location. The wandering Jew leaves will last throughout the summer and autumn until frost. To encourage a continuous show of white blooms from the small-flowered begonia, place this pair of wooden troughs in bright shade, beside a water feature where they can benefit from the humidity.

◆ GROWING TIPS ◆

Plant the troughs after the chance of frost has passed. Feed the plants every two weeks to encourage healthy leaves and flowers. Keep wandering Jew plants bushy by pinching out the growing tips of over-long shoots. Both wooden trough plantings will last through the summer months and until the onset of the first autumn frosts.

WANDERING JEW
Zebrina pendula has fleshy stems and is a fast-growing, trailing perennial.
Six plants. •

For indoor container plantings, grow wandering Jew in very bright light. Growth becomes messy and straggly
• *if the light level is too low.*

Wooden trough, •
9in (23cm) deep,
28in (70cm) wide.

BEGONIA
Begonia semperflorens
'Coco Ducolor' is one
of the most popular and
reliable of summer bedding
plants. Five plants. •

*Purple-bronze leaves
echo the color of the
wandering Jew foliage.* •

• *Wooden trough;
12in (30cm) deep,
18in (45cm) wide.*

Treat the wood with •
*preservative. Avoid
using creosote, which
is harmful to plants.*

Height
27in
(68cm)

DECKS OF DELIGHT

ALPINE BOWLS (*Left*)
A shady platform on a flight of wooden garden steps is a good spot for low bowls of alpines, such as stonecrops and hens and chicks. The huge, spiked leaves of gunnera introduce textural interest, while brilliant 'Red Emperor' mimulus adds a welcome dash of color to capture your attention.

CENTER STAGE (*Right*)
A weathered terracotta pot is filled with brilliant red nasturtiums and apricot verbena, a combination that looks particularly effective in its sunny position against the vivid green grape leaves that clamber over the rail of the deck patio. (See p.72 for details.)

BOARDWALK (*Below*)
In summer, a stepped deck leading up to a sheltered veranda provides a flower-filled platform for trumpets of sweet-scented white tobacco plants, terracotta pots of pale pink snapdragons, a hanging basket of flowering geraniums, and low bowls planted with impatiens and shocking pink verbena.

ORNAMENTAL GRASSES FOR SPECIAL USES
& SEED HEAD ATTRACTIVENESS

The following chart shows ornamental grasses that have special uses and the time period when these ornamental grasses have attractive seed heads. This information was recorded from plants grown at Longwood Gardens.

DROUGHT TOLERANT	SEED HEAD DATES
Andropogon gerardii Big Bluestem	September - December
Andropogon virginicus Broom-sedge	September - November
Bouteloua curtipendula Side-oats Grama	July - November
Calamagrostis × *acutiflora* **cv. Karl Foerster** Feather-reed Grass	June - February
Miscanthus sinensis **cv. Gracillimus** Maiden Grass	September - February
Panicum virgatum (and most cultivars) Switch Grass	July - March
WET SITE TOLERANT	
Arundo donax Giant Reed	September - November
Deschampsia cespitosa **cv. Schottland** Scottish Tufted Hair Grass	July - August
Miscanthus sinensis (most cultivars) Miscanthus	September - February
Phalaris arundinacea **cv. Picta and cv. Feesey** Ribbon Grass and Feesey's Ribbon Grass	June - August
CUT FLOWER USE	
Andropogon elliottii Elliott's Broom-sedge	September - November
Andropogon gerardii Big Bluestem	September - December
Briza media Quaking Grass	May - June
Erianthus alopecuroides Silver Plume Grass	September - March
Miscanthus (all species and cultivars) Miscanthus	September - February
Pennisetum (all species and cultivars) Fountain Grass	July - October

Large - Leaved Glory Bush ✗

For plant sources, please refer to the blue "Plant Source Information" boxes located throughout the Idea Garden.

Copyright © 1998 Longwood Gardens, Inc.
PO Box 501, Kennett Square, PA 19348-0501
610-388-1000
www.longwoodgardens.org

Printed on recycled paper.

Longwood Gardens

ORNAMENTAL GRASSES
Idea Garden Information Sheet

WHAT ARE ORNAMENTAL GRASSES?

All grasses are highly specialized plants which grow from the base up, rather than producing new growth at the tip of the stem. Ornamental grasses occur as perennial and annual grasses and are grown for their various ornamental features which include summer and fall foliage color; flower color, texture and form; and overall plant size and habit. There are two different growth habits: clump forming and spreading. Both habits spread by underground rhizomes but spreading grasses also grow by above ground stolons. Clump forming grasses spread and increase in size more slowly while spreading types can be more aggressive and spread quicker than clump forming.

USE, CULTURE, AND CARE OF ORNAMENTAL GRASSES

Ornamental grasses provide the garden with dramatic changes throughout the growing season and offer a variety of uses such as ground cover, screening, specimen, or container plants. Many grasses are fast growing and will give immediate landscape effects after only one growing season. Through careful selection, you can find ornamental grasses suitable for tough planting situations including sites in shade or full sun and wet or dry soils.

For neater appearance, the plants should be cut back once a year. Early spring before new growth appears is best. Cutting 3 to 6" from the ground is adequate and would provide space for an interplanting of early spring bulbs.

Most selected cultivars are propagated by division. Grass clumps may be lifted from the ground and divided with a spade. Most ornamental grasses are easily divided in spring. Older clumps left undivided may eventually begin to die out in the center and become unsightly. Replacing with divisions taken from the outside of these clumps will renew the plant.

1. Original plant
2. Lift
3. Divide
4. Replant

EXAMPLE GARDEN
Idea Garden Information Sheet

The Example Garden features plants from each of the eleven other display areas in the Idea Garden. Within the Example Garden there are two distinct areas, the Urban and the Suburban Gardens, which have been developed to display plants and garden structures. Many displays in the Example Garden reflect components of ecological gardening (Eco-gardening). Look throughout the garden for this symbol, 🌍 to learn more about Eco-gardening.

MULCH

Plants, especially newly planted ones, benefit from mulch. Mulch is anything that is spread over the soil around the base of the plant. Common organic mulches are wood chips, leaves, or hay. Mulch serves many functions:
- Reduces weed germination and growth
- Improves water infiltration by preventing the soil from crusting
- Retains soil moisture
- Keeps soil cooler in the summer
- Encourages fibrous root development
- Protects the trunks of trees or shrubs from lawn mower damage
- Improves soil quality
- Reduces splashing of mud onto plant leaves and flowers

Usually two to four inches of mulch that extends well beyond the original planting hole are all that are needed to provide these benefits. It is advisable to maintain a suitable mulch for several years after transplanting. Avoid applying too much mulch, especially right up against trunks or stems, which may provide a good home for insects in the summer or rodents in the winter.

CULTURAL PRACTICES

An environmentally friendly landscape can begin with some simple changes in technique. In addition to having a positive effect on the landscape, many of these practices can make our gardening chores easier.
- Select varieties of turfgrass that are disease resistant and drought tolerant. Look for ones that have been bred to retain a deep green color with less fertilizer.

(continued on back)

- Use slow-release organic fertilizers. These last longer and provide steady nutrition for the plant.

- Conserve moisture by selecting drought tolerant plants, using mulch to conserve moisture, and using soaker hoses or drip irrigation to put water only where it is needed and avoid loss due to evaporation.

- Encourage beneficial insects to help control harmful pests.

- Birds, bats, and toads also eat insects. Encourage them to visit your garden by providing shelter and water.

CREATING A HEALTHIER ENVIRONMENT AT LONGWOOD

Longwood Gardens is committed to sound environmental management practices. Some of our efforts include: a garden-wide Integrated Pest Management (IPM) program, a bluebird habitat project, a wetlands enhancement project, a state-of-the-art sewage treatment plant, energy conservation systems in our conservatories and throughout the gardens, a recycling program for the offices and Terrace Restaurant, and an extensive composting and soil renewal program.

SOURCES FOR BENEFICIAL INSECTS

(No endorsement of named companies is intended, nor is criticism implied of similar companies that are not mentioned.)

Alternative Garden Supply Inc.
297 North Barrington Rd.
Streamwood, IL 60107

Bozeman Bio-Tech Inc.
Box 3146
Bozeman, MT 59772
800-289-6656

Foothill Agricultural Research
510 West Chase Dr.
Corona, CA 91720

Gardens Alive!
PO Box 149
Sunman, IN 47041
812-537-8650

Harmony Farm Supply and Nursery
PO Box 460
Graton, CA 95444
707-823-9125

IPM Laboratories, Inc.
Main Street
Locke, NY 13092-0099
315-497-2063

Nature's Control
PO Box 35
Medford, OR 97501
503-899-8318

Necessary Trading Company
PO Box 305
New Castle, VA 24127
703-864-5103

Peaceful Valley Farm Supply
Box 2209
Grass Valley, CA 95945
916-272-4769

Rincon-Ritova Insectaries, Inc.
PO Box 95
Oak View, CA 93022
805-643-5407

For plant sources, please refer to the blue "Plant Source Information" boxes located throughout the Idea Garden.

SUN-LOVING NASTURTIUMS

☀ SUN 🍴 MEDIUM-RICH POTTING MIX 🌱 MOIST CONDITIONS

LONG-LASTING, vivid scarlet flowers combined with decorative trailing foliage make nasturtiums a very popular choice for container plantings. Here they are planted simply but effectively with 'Peaches and Cream' verbena whose densely packed, lightly scented florets contrast with the bolder nasturtium flowerheads. The verbena was introduced fairly recently and has a subtle, light perfume similar to apricots. If you are unable to find this variety at garden centers, use a pink verbena such as 'Silver Ann' instead.

♦ GROWING TIPS ♦

Plant the pot in early summer. Check the nasturtium leaves and flowers periodically for signs of black aphid infestation, and spray them with a mixture of water and dishwashing liquid. Verbenas are susceptible to mildew, so ensure that the soil is moist but not soggy when watering.

Nasturtiums will flower profusely ♦ without feeding.

NASTURTIUM ♦
Tropaeolum majus 'Empress of India' is a sun-loving, fast-growing annual. Five plants.

Pastryware terracotta pot, ♦ 12in (30cm) deep, 15in (38cm) wide.

♦ **VERBENA**
Verbena 'Peaches and Cream' bears primroselike flowers arranged in large clusters. Four plants.

Height 28in (70cm)

BED OF MARIGOLDS

☀ SUN   🔨 MEDIUM-RICH POTTING MIX   ✌ MOIST CONDITIONS

A GOLDEN BED OF AFRICAN MARIGOLDS, blanket flowers, and coleus is shown off to best advantage in this low wooden trough. I've planted orange-colored African marigolds and blanket flowers in rows at opposite ends of the container, and added gold- and lime-green-colored coleus between the two. As a rule, planting in straight rows should be avoided but, in this display, it helps to distinguish between flower types that share similar coloring. For maximum impact, site this predominantly orange planting near deep red or yellow flowers and foliage in the garden. Hot colors such as these can also look interesting adjacent to pale pink flowers.

◆ GROWING TIPS ◆

Plant the trough in mild weather toward the end of spring. Deadhead marigolds and blanket flowers regularly to encourage them to produce even more flowers. To achieve the best green and gold leaf color from the coleus plants, remove flower spikes and take out longer-growing shoots to keep the plants bushy. Feed the display at least once every two weeks.

BLANKET FLOWER
Gaillardia x grandiflora 'Dazzler'
has daisylike red flowers that last
for several months. Five plants. ●

COLEUS
Coleus blumei is grown
for its attractively colored
and patterned leaves.
Three plants. ●

Height
22in
(55cm)

AFRICAN MARIGOLD
Tagetes erecta grows
well in an open site.
Eight plants. ●

● *Wooden trough,*
8in (20cm) deep,
29in (74cm) wide.

TRAILING CONVOLVULUS

☀ SUN   🛠 MEDIUM-RICH POTTING MIX   🏺 MOIST CONDITIONS

ONVOLVULUS, WITH ITS MASS of vibrant purple-blue flowers, is a good choice for container gardeners because, with just three plants, you can create a full display. This actual planting has survived for four years and each year produces an incredibly impressive show of flowers. In my experience, *Convolvulus sabatius* is the most reliable plant of the convolvulus group for growing in containers; *Convolvulus tricolor* tends to become straggly and *Convolvulus althaeoides* simply does not grow well in pots. Position this planting on a sunny deck or paved area where it can be viewed in all its splendid glory.

◆ GROWING TIPS ◆

Plant the container in spring. Cut back all the flowers after their first flush. For best results, feed the display every few weeks with a liquid tomato plant fertilizer. Pests do not seem to be a problem. Convolvulus can also withstand light frost, but shelter the planting from cold in winter months.

CONVOLVULUS
Convolvulus sabatius flowers in summer and early autumn.
• Three plants.

The flowers open up each morning and close again in the early evening.

Leaf display continues until late autumn.

Terracotta pot; 13in (34cm) deep, 16in (40cm) wide.

Height
22in
(55cm)

PASTEL PALETTE

☀ SUN 🖌 MEDIUM-RICH POTTING MIX ⚗ MOIST CONDITIONS

COLOR PLAYS an important part in this planting. Rich creamy yellow osteospermum flowers are juxtaposed with brilliant pink ivy geraniums, the colors of which are subtly picked up by green-, pink-, and white-striped tradescantia leaves. I was once told that mixing yellow and pink is a great sin, in which case I am a great sinner, for I love to pair up these pastel colors. This mix, grown in a sunny position on a deck, terrace, or patio, will look fresh and sunny through the summer months.

◆ GROWING TIPS ◆

Plant up the display in early summer. To encourage the maximum number of new flowers, deadhead both the geraniums and osteospermum on a regular basis. Whereas geraniums produce an unending show of color, osteospermums produce waves of blooms throughout the summer.

OSTEOSPERMUM
Osteospermum 'Buttermilk' has aromatic leaves.
Three plants. ●

IVY GERANIUM
Pelargonium peltatum 'Crocodile'.
Three plants. ●

TRADESCANTIA
Tradescantia fluminensis 'Albovittata' is an attractive frost-tender evergreen.
Three plants. ●

An upright habit is characteristic of this ● semiwoody plant.

● *White wooden windowbox; 12in (30cm) deep, 24in (60cm) wide.*

Height
27in
(68cm)

PAVED PATIOS

HERB SELECTION (Far Left)
A sunny south-facing wall is a perfect site for growing herbs. Here, a vegetable rack lined with moss makes an interesting three-tier planter. (See pp. 78-79 for details.)

MIX AND MATCH (Left)
An eclectic mix of plant shapes is brought together in this attractive grouping of pots. The display includes fleshy-leaved succulents, marguerites, geraniums, and a cordyline with its fountain of dark coppery leaves.

COPPER CAULDRON (Below Left)
A copper tub, left to stand, will develop a delicious blue-green patina, and it looks superb planted with lilac petunias, feathery purple heliotrope, pink diascia, and catmint.

LILAC URN (Below Right)
Fragrant lilac heliotrope and the blue daisies of felicia are perfectly matched in an elegant classically shaped terracotta urn.

AROMATIC HERB RACK

☀ SUN   🍴 MEDIUM-RICH POTTING MIX   ⚱ MOIST CONDITIONS

A MULTISTORY CONTAINER is ideal for housing a selection of culinary herbs in a small garden because you can grow three times as many plants as usual in a restricted space. I have made the planting decorative as well as practical by including scented geraniums (their leaves can be used to flavor ice cream or cakes) among the more traditional culinary herbs: parsley, sage, thyme, basil, chives, and marjoram. Many of these popular herbs have a Mediterranean origin and are therefore sun-loving. A sunny paved area outside the kitchen door makes a perfect location for this aromatic herb rack.

◆ GROWING TIPS ◆

Plant the herbs in spring in a tall wire rack that allows good drainage. Line each pocket of the rack with moss and heavy-duty plastic. Pierce plenty of holes for drainage in the plastic and fill each pocket of the wire rack with medium-rich potting mix. The herb plantings will last for several years. If the mixed herbs in the smaller terracotta pots become too crowded, divide them in spring.

CHIVES
Allium schoenoprasum has a mild onion flavor and carries globular mauve flowers in spring. Two plants.

OREGANO
Origanum vulgare 'Curly Gold' bears savory flavored leaves that scorch in direct sunlight. One plant.

GOLDEN VARIEGATED SAGE
Salvia officinalis 'Icterina' has a milder flavor than common sage and is popular with bees. One plant.

LEMON THYME
Thymus x citriodorus 'Aureus' is a hardy plant, noted for its lemon-scented leaves. One plant.

Height
43in
(107cm)

◆ Terracotta pot,
8in (20cm) deep,
5in (12cm) wide.

DARK OPAL BASIL ●
*Ocimum basilicum 'Dark Opal',
a native of India, is often placed
on windowsills to deter flies.*
Four plants.

GOLDEN THYME
*Thymus 'Doone Valley' has a
lemon scent. Pick leaves in summer
when the plant is in bloom.*
One plant. ●

SCENTED GERANIUM
*Pelargonium crispum
'Variegatum'. Rub the
scented leaves to release
their tangy fragrance.*
One plant. ●

SCENTED GERANIUM
*Pelargonium x fragrans
bears attractive leaves
with a spicy pine
flavor.* One plant. ●

POT MARJORAM
*Origanum onites has dark
green peppery flavored
leaves and small pale pink
flowers.* One plant.

SCENTED GERANIUM
*'Letitia' is a tender plant
and needs replacing each
spring.* One plant.

THYME
*Thymus doerfleri
has aromatic silver
leaves and pale
pink flowers.*
● Two plants.

CURLED PARSLEY
*Petroselinum crispum
grows well in most
containers. Place
parsley next to rose
shrubs to improve
their scent.* Three
● plants.

● *Wire rack
lined with
green moss
and plastic;
30in (75cm)
high, 10in
(25cm) wide.*

PETUNIA BASKET

☀ SUN/SEMISHADE　🔱 MEDIUM-RICH POTTING MIX　🗹 MOIST CONDITIONS

SMALL CONTAINERS call for diminutive plants and flowers that will not overwhelm one another or the proportions of the pot. Here, a latticework terracotta basket is filled with a vibrant mix of pink and red flowers. Coral pink geraniums are teamed up with vivid red phlox, pink petunias, and dusty pink clusters of polygonum flowers, all offset by a variety of leaves. Place this eye-catching arrangement in a bright but sheltered location.

◆ GROWING TIPS ◆

Plant the basket in early summer. Deadhead petunias, geraniums, and phlox regularly to encourage new flowers, and feed the display every two weeks with a high-phosphorus liquid fertilizer. Take geranium cuttings in late summer and then overwinter them in a frost-free site.

PETUNIA
Petunia Resisto Series 'Brick' *has particularly resilient flowers that are undamaged by rain.*
● One plant.

ZONAL GERANIUM
Pelargonium 'Frank Headley' *is an attractive cream- and green-leaved variety with pink flowers.* Two plants. ●

POLYGONUM
Polygonum 'Victory Carpet'. *A variety with a low, trailing habit.* Two plants. ●

PHLOX
Phlox drummondii 'Fantasy Mixed'. *A bushy annual with pale pink flowers.* One plant.

Height 16in (40cm)

● *Latticework basket; 10in (25cm) deep, 16in (40cm) wide.*

OASIS GARDEN

☼ BRIGHT SHADE 🏺 MEDIUM-RICH POTTING MIX AND GRIT 🗲 DRY CONDITIONS

A BOWL OF SUCCULENTS can provide a welcome oasis in your living room or kitchen, and the variety of natural forms and colors common to these evergreen plants offers year-round interest. Some succulents produce a few sparse leaves, others fleshy leaves, while some have no leaves at all. They all make excellent houseplants since they have adapted to growing in dry, inhospitable areas and therefore require very little maintenance. Succulents produce a number of babies and side shoots that you can remove from the parent and plant in a new arrangement.

◆ GROWING TIPS ◆

Succulents are best planted in spring or summer in a mixture of equal parts medium-rich potting mix and fine grit. Keep the bowl planting on the dry side. Even in rooms with central heating, succulents require watering only once every two to three weeks. Good drainage is essential.

CRASSULA
Crassula lycopodioides has tall, leafless stems branching from its base. One plant.

SENECIO
Senecio kleinii. One plant.

HAWORTHIA
Haworthia attenuata 'Clariperla' is a clump-forming succulent. Two plants.

ECHEVERIA
Echeveria harmsii grows wild from Texas south to Argentina. One plant.

SENECIO
Senecio articulata bears white or red brushlike flowers. One plant.

• *China bowl, 5in (12cm) deep, 16in (40cm) wide.*

GASTERIA •
Gasteria verrucosa is an easy-to-grow, stemless succulent. One plant.

Height
14in
(36cm)

FLOWER AND FERN DISPLAY

☼ SHADE/SEMISHADE ◆ ACIDIC POTTING MIX ⌂ MOIST CONDITIONS

F RESH GREEN FERN LEAVES marry beautifully with clear yellow begonias and
lilac-blue hydrangeas in this lead planter. In a horizontal display, the
shapes and textures of flowers and foliage take on great importance. Fronds
of maidenhair fern and hard shield fern offset the large, smooth leaves of
begonias and hydrangeas, while the compact, roselike begonia flowers
complement the frothy hydrangea mopheads. Position the
planter in a sheltered site along the edge
of a patio, next to a wall, or against
a backdrop of taller ferns.

HYDRANGEA
Hydrangea macrophylla
'Générale Vicomtesse
de Vibraye' *prefers a sheltered
site. An acidic soil produces lilac-
blue bracts that flower for three
months. Two plants.* •

MAIDENHAIR FERN
*Adiantum raddianum is a
commonly cultivated fern. It
likes to be watered frequently
and dislikes direct sunlight.*
Two plants. •

Antique lead planter; •
*6in (15cm) deep,
4ft (1.2m) long.*

◆ GROWING TIPS ◆

Plant the lead container after the chance of frost has passed. During autumn, plant out the hard shield ferns and hydrangeas in the garden. Before the first autumn frosts, bring tender maidenhair ferns and begonias indoors. Stop watering the begonia plants completely so that they dry off. Carefully remove their yellow foliage and store the begonia tubers in almost-dry fibrous peat until spring, when you can plant them out.

Height
25in
(63cm)

BEGONIA
Begonia x tuberhybrida 'Festiva'
is a tuberous begonia producing double
bright yellow blooms from early to late
◆ *summer*. Two plants.

HARD SHIELD FERN
Polystichum aculeatum
is often found growing in
woodland areas by water.
Three plants. ◆

◆ *Large green*
hydrangea leaves
help to soften the
horizontal edges
of the container.

POTS FOR PERGOLAS

RUSTIC RETREAT (Left)
A rustic loggia bathed in afternoon sun is a perfect place to sit and admire this magnificent fuchsia 'Countess of Maritza' circled by a ruff of impatiens. (See p.87 for details.)

SHADY PERGOLA (Right)
In an oasis of late-summer green, beneath a canopy of white, scented jasmine, stands a monumental terracotta pot of 'Ashford Red' abutilon. These bell-shaped flowers are produced for several months throughout the summer and are echoed by the bloodleaf in the small pot. (See p.86 and p.109 for details.)

CLASSICAL LOGGIA (Below)
Spiraled boxwood trees in pots, and half barrels planted with bay standards, enhance the architectural beauty of this classical loggia.

Towering Abutilon

☀ SUN   ⚒ MEDIUM-RICH POTTING MIX   ⚱ MOIST CONDITIONS

A BUTILONS ARE REWARDING PLANTS because in a single season they may grow several feet high and are covered in flowers from midsummer until the first autumn frosts. The varieties of abutilon that do best in containers are all frost tender. *Abutilon* x *hybridum* 'Ashford Red', used in this display, carries bell-shaped salmon-red flowers, but orange, pink, yellow, and white varieties are also available. The hardiest variety, *Abutilon* x *suntense*, has lilac or white flowers and blooms in spring and early summer. The monumental scale of abutilons makes them a dramatic choice for a sunny but sheltered arbor, pergola, or loggia.

Bamboo stakes support •
growing abutilon stems.

◆ Growing Tips ◆

Plant the pot after the chance of frost has passed. Prune the growing tips when the stems are about 3ft (1m) high. Stake the plants as they grow to prevent them from blowing over in high winds. The lower stems of abutilon can be bare, so grow a mat-forming plant such as *Sagina glabra* 'Aurea' around the stem base. Throughout the growing season feed weekly, and keep well watered.

ABUTILON
Abutilon x *hybridum*
'Ashford Red' *carries a profusion of bell-shaped flowers for several months.*
• Three plants.

Height
4ft
(1.2m)

PEARLWORT •
Sagina glabra 'Aurea'
produces hummocks of gold-green foliage.
Seven plants.

• *Terracotta basin,*
14in (35cm) deep,
30in (75cm) wide.

CASCADING FUCHSIA CANOPY

☼ BRIGHT SHADE   ⚱ RICH POTTING MIX   ⚒ MOIST CONDITIONS

A STANDARD FUCHSIA swathed in flowers is a truly amazing sight. The best standards are produced by varieties of fuchsia that have semipendulous growth, such as 'Swingtime', 'Voodoo', 'Pink Galore', and 'Winston Churchill'. Plant similarly colored New Guinea or standard impatiens around the foot of the standard in colors that echo those of the fuchsias. Impatiens are the perfect companion plants for fuchsias because they thrive in exactly the same growing conditions and cover up the bare stem of the standard. A sheltered arbor or loggia makes a good site, since most fuchsia standards dislike windy locations and prefer bright shade.

FUCHSIA ●
Fuchsia hybrid. The drooping habit of many varieties makes them good choices. One plant.

◆ GROWING TIPS ◆

It is fairly straightforward to train a standard fuchsia (*see p.151.*) Ideally, start in autumn, two years before you want flowers, and grow the plant in a frost-free environment. With strong varieties such as this, the stem of the standard will thicken by 1-2in (2.5-5cm) and produce a reasonable-sized flowering head in the second spring. Its main flowering will be in spring and again in autumn.

Height
5ft
(1.5m)

Square, chrysanthemum-motif terracotta pot;
16in (40cm) deep
16in (40cm) wide. ●

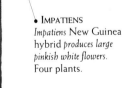

● IMPATIENS
Impatiens New Guinea hybrid *produces large pinkish white flowers.* Four plants.

SUMMER STRIPES

☀ SUN/SEMISHADE   🔱 MEDIUM-RICH POTTING MIX   ⚒ MOIST CONDITIONS

PETUNIAS AND ZONAL GERANIUMS both have a long and
bountiful flowering season, which makes them a popular
choice for summer container plantings. Here, crimson-pink
and white-striped petunias are mixed with deep pink
geraniums to produce a wonderfully vibrant
effect. In addition, the pale silver-and-
green-striped leaves of tradescantia
foliage echo the pattern on the
petunia petals. In the perfect
position, standing guard at
the entrance to an arbor or
pergola, this easily grown
planting makes a bold,
colorful statement.

PETUNIA •
Petunia x *hybrida* Star Series
flowers for up to four months.
Three plants per pot.

PETUNIA •
Petunia x *hybrida*
Star Series *needs full
sun to give of its best.*

Height
3ft
(1m)

◆ GROWING TIPS ◆

Plant the pots once the chance of
frost has passed. Deadhead petunias
frequently to encourage the plants to
produce the maximum number of
blooms. Cut back flowering stems
halfway through the growing season
if the plants start to become leggy.
Feed on a weekly basis with a high-
phosphorus liquid fertilizer.

ZONAL GERANIUM
*Pelargonium 'Sterling Stent' is
a prolific flowerer. This variety has
a dark circular zone on each leaf.*
Three plants per pot. ●

TRADESCANTIA
*Tradescantia fluminensis
'Quicksilver' has thin, almost
transparent, leaves, the undersides of
which appear purple in bright light.*
● Three plants per pot.

● *Reconstituted stone pot;
15in (38cm) deep,
10in (25cm) wide.*

WINDOW DISPLAYS

WINDOW OF OPPORTUNITY (*Far Left*)
A shaded windowsill plays host to a small terracotta windowbox planted with yellow and orange tuberous begonias, yellow and white pansies, and pink double impatiens. All will flower throughout the summer and autumn. (*See pp.94-95 for details.*)

PERFECT PANSIES (*Left*)
In early spring, a collection of small pots filled with Universal Series white pansies creates a welcoming display on a window ledge.

BEHIND BARS (*Below*)
Bars at the window to keep intruders at bay become less of an eyesore when hidden behind a floriferous planting of swan river daisies, scaevola, and the trailing silver foliage of artemisia. (*See pp.92-93 for details.*)

FEATHERY FILIGREE

☀ SUN/SEMISHADE 🖌 MEDIUM-RICH POTTING MIX ⚱ MOIST CONDITIONS

S WAN RIVER DAISIES AND SCAEVOLA are two summer-flowering annuals
that are becoming increasingly popular. These swan river daisies have
filigrees of tiny leaves surmounted by bushy crowns of blue daisy flowers
with bright yellow centers. *Scaevola emula* produces long spikes
of lilac-blue flowers that last until the first frosts. They work well
together visually since the delicacy of one balances the coarseness
of the other; luckily they enjoy the same conditions.
   In this planting, swan river daisy and scaevola are
joined by *Artemisia* 'Silver Brocade'. All three plants
grow vigorously and have a low-growing habit
which makes them a good choice for a
windowbox or trough. They will
thrive in the limited space of a
container, spilling over the
edges to form a full display.

ARTEMISIA •──────
Artemisia 'Silver Brocade'
has abundant, aromatic,
silver-gray foliage.
Two plants.

◆ GROWING TIPS ◆
Plant the windowbox after the
chance of frost has passed. Don't
worry about deadheading the daisies
or scaevola, but remove the long
flowering stems of the artemisia
to encourage bushy growth.
Feed all the plants with a high-
phosphorus liquid fertilizer
every two weeks.

Height
25in
(64cm)

SWAN RIVER DAISY
Brachycome iberidifolia
continues to flower well
into the autumn months.
● Three plants.

● **SCAEVOLA**
Scaevola emula is an Australian
plant. It is a fast-growing, long-
flowering annual. Three plants.

Ever-gray artemisia
can be used to form
the foundation of
● *many plantings.*

● *Rustic wooden trough,*
16in (40cm) deep,
25in (64cm) long.

SHADY TRIO

☀ SHADE/SEMISHADE 🌡 MEDIUM-RICH POTTING MIX ⚱ MOIST CONDITIONS

ORANGE, PRIMROSE YELLOW, and ice pink flowers are brought
together in this terracotta windowbox to produce one of my all
time favorite color mixes. Double-flowered impatiens, pansies, and
begonias make good companions and are particularly useful plants
for container gardeners because they will flourish in shady sites.
Impatiens have been widely hybridized, and this double-
flowered type produces enormous quantities of
pale pink, roselike flowers. Display this
glorious planting on a sheltered window
ledge to brighten up an area that doesn't
receive much direct sunlight.

PANSY •
Viola x wittrockiana 'Antique
Shades' *comes in a range of
colors; here I've selected a plant
with pale primrose yellow
flowers.* Two plants.

*Large, serrate-edged
begonia leaves add
textural interest.* •

◆ GROWING TIPS ◆
All the plants in the display (except
pansies) are tender, so in cold areas
plant the windowbox after the
chance of frost has passed. Remove
fleshy begonia flowers that drop
inside the windowbox because they
can cause rotting if they lie against
the leaves and stems within the
planting. Deadhead the pansy
flowers regularly, and cut back
straggly stems to encourage healthy,
substantial new flower growth.

PANSY •
*Viola x wittrockiana
'Paper White' works
well in containers as a
filler plant or main
feature, in semishade or
full sun.* One plant.

IMPATIENS
Impatiens Rosette Series
offers roselike, pink flowers.
● Three plants.

BEGONIA
Begonia x *tuberhybrida*
'Non-Stop Orange'
*is a variety that lives up
to its promising name.*
● Three plants.

● *Griffin-patterned
terracotta windowbox;
8in (20cm) deep,
18in (45cm) long.*

Height
20in
(50cm)

VIBRANT VERBENA

☀ SUN | MEDIUM-RICH POTTING MIX   ⚱ MOIST CONDITIONS

CREATE A SHIMMERING basket of scarlet and crimson by growing red verbena and phlox flowers against a dark background of red-veined polygonum leaves and trails of dark green English ivy. I have chosen this variety of verbena for its subtle fragrance and for the sparkly white centers of its vivid flowers. Hanging baskets brimming with bright color are ideal for livening up a bare wall, or for suspending from the horizontal beam of an arbor or pergola. With frequent watering and deadheading, this colorful planting will flower through the summer.

◆ GROWING TIPS ◆

Plant the basket in early summer. In hot weather, water the display twice a day. Feed the plants weekly with a high-phosphorus liquid fertilizer, and deadhead regularly. Verbena is prone to mildew during hot, dry spells. Spray the contents of the hanging basket from time to time with fungicide to prevent infection.

PHLOX
Phlox drummondii comes in a brilliant selection of colors. Four plants.

POLYGONUM
Polygonum 'Victory Carpet' also grows well in rock gardens or on banks. Four plants.

Moss-filled wire basket; 6in (15cm) deep, 16in (40cm) wide.

VERBENA
Verbena x hybrida 'Defiance' flowers profusely from early summer to the first frosts. Five plants.

ENGLISH IVY
Hedera helix 'Ivalace' is a small-leaved form, suitable for indoor plantings. Four plants.

Height
26in
(65cm)

SKEINS OF GOLD

☀ BRIGHT SHADE ⚱ MEDIUM-RICH POTTING MIX ⚲ MOIST CONDITIONS

FOR A FRESH green and yellow hanging basket
throughout the summer, combine lysimachia
and tradescantia foliage with bright yellow
oxalis and cosmos flowers. You could also try
English ivies in a range of leaf colors and
shapes for a similar effect, or use variegated
cream and green *Vinca major* 'Variegata',
which has long trailing stems, or the gold
and silver variegated forms of *Helichrysum
petiolare*. Position this natural-looking
arrangement in bright shade where
lysimachia, tradescantia, and
oxalis will be most at home.

◆ GROWING TIPS ◆
Plant the hanging basket in early
summer. Cut back the cosmos plants
to prevent them looking too straggly.
Feed the display twice a week with a
high-phosphorus liquid fertilizer to
encourage flowering. Water liberally
to prevent the planting from drying
out, especially during hot weather.

TRADESCANTIA ●
Tradescantia fluminensis 'Variegata',
*with its attractive striped leaves, makes
an excellent trailing plant for hanging
baskets. Four plants.*

OXALIS ●
*Oxalis lobata is a dainty,
low-growing plant with
distinctive red stems.
Four plants.*

● *Wire basket,
6in (15cm) deep,
16in (40cm) wide.*

Height
3ft
(1m)

LYSIMACHIA ●
Lysimachia nummularia 'Aurea'
*produces trails of golden leaves
that grow up to 6ft (2m) in length.
Three plants.*

COSMOS ●
Cosmos 'Sunny Gold'
*has a long season of
flowers if deadheaded
regularly. Three plants.*

PLANTS FOR PATHWAYS

WINTER BERRIES (*Left*)
In autumn, hardy wintergreen and juniper are planted in a low, tarnished copper bowl to create a shimmering planting on a red brick path. (*See pp. 132-133 for details.*)

COLORFUL INTERLUDE (*Right*)
A stone urn brimming with luscious, waxy pink impatiens, ageratum, and tiny silver-leaved plectostachys forms a pool of color against a backdrop of evergreen boxwood and honeysuckle. (*See p. 100 for details.*)

COBBLED PATH (*Below*)
Throughout summer, the delicate purple-blue flowers of streptocarpus sit between pots of geraniums on a cobbled path. Daisylike marguerite and felicia flowers, plectostachys, and shrubby solanum sit directly behind.

FROTHY PINKS AND LILACS

☀ SEMISHADE 🔨 MEDIUM-RICH POTTING MIX 🥄 MOIST CONDITIONS

A LOW URN overflowing with ageratum, impatiens, and silver-leaved plectostachys makes an impressive display. The range of flower color is limited to a soft palette of lilac, pale pink, and rich pink, framed by a froth of silver-gray foliage. To do its best, ageratum needs to be kept very moist. Luckily, impatiens enjoy growing in similar conditions and, although plectostachys plants prefer dry soil, they still perform well in this arrangement. Stand the urn on a path where it can be seen from several viewpoints.

◆ GROWING TIPS ◆

Plant the urn in early summer since impatiens, ageratum, and plectostachys are frost tender. Well-drained potting mix is important because, although ageratum and impatiens like moist soil, they dislike being waterlogged.

IMPATIENS
Impatiens New Guinea hybrid
*in a blend of pale and cyclamen
• pink flowers.* Three plants.

AGERATUM
*Ageratum houstonianum
'Bengali' originates from
Mexico and bears clusters
of long-lasting, lilac-blue
• flowers.* Three plants.

PLECTOSTACHYS
*Plectostachys serphyllifolia is a
tender evergreen with trails of tiny
silver leaves. It makes an attractive
alternative to helichrysum.*
Three plants. •

Weathered stone urn; •
16in (40cm) high, 24in (60cm) wide.

Height
26in
(65cm)

HOT COMBINATION

☀ SUN 🗴 RICH POTTING MIX ⬨ MOIST CONDITIONS

LANTANA, WITH ITS SMALL, clustered flowers in a number of hot color mixes such as pink and yellow, orange and pink, or scarlet and orange, makes a fantastically vibrant container planting. It grows prolifically, so much so that in many tropical countries it is regarded as a weed. Lantana is a poisonous plant, though not deadly, and the aromatic dark green leaves have a strange odor when rubbed between the fingers. Stand a pair of urns brimming with lantana, ornamental coleus foliage, and trailing ivy on either side of a path to create a formal entrance.

◆ GROWING TIPS ◆

Plant the stone urns after the chance of frost since lantana and coleus are frost tender. Keep both plants bushy by pinching out straggly growth, and remove the coleus' flower spikes.

Height
3ft
(1m)

COLEUS
Coleus blumei, a striking plant from Java, bears leaves in many color patterns. Two plants. •

LANTANA
Lantana camara bears flowers that often darken with age so that you see two or more colors in one • flowerhead. Four plants.

ENGLISH IVY •
Hedera helix 'Glacier' has trails of variegated silver leaves that are frost hardy. Four plants.

Spiral-grooved, •
*reconstituted stone urn;
24in (60cm) deep,
16in (40cm) wide.*

BOLD BLOCKS OF COLOR

☀ SUN/BRIGHT SHADE   ⚒ MEDIUM-RICH POTTING MIX   ⚱ MOIST CONDITIONS

W E THINK OF IMPATIENS as shade-loving plants and geraniums as sun-lovers; however, they can coexist quite happily in a variety of conditions. The smaller of these two square terracotta pots is planted with both scarlet and pink geraniums. The larger pot has the same type of rich salmon pink geranium, 'Playboy Speckles', and a scarlet red impatiens with distinctively striped bronze leaves. Place the terracotta pots as a pair on the edge of a path where their startling caps of color can be viewed to full advantage. Avoid very deep shade or hot, exposed sites, which neither impatiens nor geraniums enjoy.

GERANIUM ●
*Pelargonium 'Orbit Red'
has dark leaves and vivid
scarlet flowers.* Three plants.

◆ GROWING TIPS ◆

Plant the pots in spring when all chance of frost has passed. A weekly feed of liquid tomato fertilizer will give you a mass of flowers for several months on end. Remember to dead-head both geraniums regularly, and remove any dying impatiens flowers that drop into the pots since they can cause rot. Watch out for aphid infestation early in the season.

Height
32in
(80cm)

Small terracotta cube; ●
*10in (25cm) deep,
10in (25cm) wide.*

In a dry, sunny site this
display will put on a reliable
show of flamboyant color
● for four to five months.

GERANIUM
Pelargonium 'Playboy Speckles'
boasts light pink flowers with
random splashes of darker color.
● Three plants.

IMPATIENS ●
Impatiens New
Guinea hybrid.
A popular choice with
variegated leaves and
brilliant red flowers.
Three plants.

● Large terracotta cube;
15in (38cm) deep,
15in (38cm) wide.

Paint the terracotta pot ●
with yogurt to encourage
moss and lichens to grow
on the surface. (See p.10
for more details.)

SUGGESTIONS FOR STEPS

RUSTIC JARS (*Left*)
In summer, a pair of salt-glazed stone jars planted with dainty purple swan river daisies and climbing akebia foliage looks at home on shallow steps. Bright yellow alchemilla plants, growing freely between the cracks in the steps, add a welcome touch of informality.

MEDITERRANEAN FLAVOR (*Right*)
At the height of summer, steps leading up to an entrance are brought to life with a row of terracotta troughs spilling over with hot pink ivy-leaved geranium flowers.

SHIMMERING PAIR (*Below Left*))
Add light to dark recesses with bowls of pale pink petunias, shimmering senecio foliage, and snapdragons. (See pp. 106-107 for details.)

SCARLET SENTINEL (*Below Right*)
A wonderful scarlet azalea stands guard at the foot of a flight of brick steps, producing a dazzling color note in late spring.

DELICATE PINKS

☀ SUN/SEMISHADE　🗲 MEDIUM-RICH POTTING MIX　🝮 MOIST CONDITIONS

TWO FLUTED TERRACOTTA BOWLS brimming with pink, red, and silver plants make a very attractive combination. Pale pink petunias and regal geraniums grow among silver foliage, and I've added red snapdragons to create a vibrant color note. Place the bowls on a flight of entrance steps to give a welcoming touch. Make sure the plantings look attractive from above as well as from the sides, and that the steps are wide enough to take the bowls comfortably and leave plenty of room to walk between them. On narrower steps, a display of several small pots, planted with colorful summer annuals, always works well.

Regal geraniums and petunia petals are easily damaged in wet and windy weather, so place the bowls in a sheltered site. ●

Fluted terracotta bowl, 8in (20cm) deep,
● *16in (40cm) wide.*

PETUNIA ●
Petunia 'Apple Blossom' is an attractive pale pink form of one of the most reliable annuals. Three plants per bowl.

◆ GROWING TIPS ◆

Plant these low bowls a little later
than most summer annual plantings
to protect tender regal geraniums
from frosts. Deadhead the petunias,
zonal geraniums, and snapdragons
regularly, and cut back leggy petunia
stems. Take cuttings from the regal
geraniums in late summer and keep
in a frost-free place. Plant out the
geraniums the following year.

SENECIO
Senecio maritima 'Silver Dust'
is an annual with fine silvery
foliage that grows quickly.
● Three plants per bowl.

REGAL GERANIUM
Pelargonium 'Lavender Grand Slam'
is a variety with white and lavender-pink
● *petals.* Two plants per bowl.

SNAPDRAGON
Antirrhinum majus 'Floral Showers'
bears fragrant red flowers and grows
exceedingly well in containers. Three
plants per bowl.

● *Fluted terracotta bowl,*
8in (20cm) deep,
23in (58cm) wide.

Height
24in
(60cm)

COOL DUO

☀ SUN/SEMISHADE 🌿 MEDIUM-RICH POTTING MIX ⚒ DRY CONDITIONS

A LOW TERRACOTTA BOWL planted with white-flowered, silver-leaved prairie gentian (*Eustoma grandiflorum*) and echeveria – a succulent with silver rosettes of fleshy leaves – presents a cool, elegant display. Prairie gentians have gained in popularity since the introduction of white, cream, purple, and pink varieties and the hybridization of smaller, carnation-like flowers. A sheltered position on a sunny patio is a suitable site for this planting, since heavy rain can damage the fragile flower petals.

◆ GROWING TIPS ◆

Echeveria is frost tender, so plant the bowl after the chance of frost has passed. Prairie gentian and echeveria prefer almost-dry soil. For the best results, feed the display every two weeks with a high-phosphorus liquid fertilizer. Bring the planting indoors over the winter months.

PRAIRIE GENTIAN
Eustoma grandiflorum 'Purple picotee' has white and purple poppylike blooms that flower throughout the summer. Four plants.

ECHEVERIA
Echeveria gibbiflora bears fleshy leaves that store water as insurance against drought. Three plants.

Low terracotta bowl, 8in (20cm) deep, 24in (60cm) wide.

Height 24in (60cm)

Take care when handling echeveria plants: the waxy leaf coating rubs off easily.

BLOODLEAF BOWL

☀ SUN/SEMISHADE 🪴 MEDIUM-RICH POTTING MIX 🌱 MOIST CONDITIONS

I N SUMMER CONTAINER PLANTINGS, it need not only be flowers that provide color. Here, bloodleaf offers a vivid contrast of gold and flame red foliage, which is exaggerated by dividing the bowl into distinct sections. Bloodleaf grows to form a mound of brilliant foliage and, for this reason, is often used to produce pattern plantings, such as the floral clocks that were so popular in Edwardian garden designs. Place the container on a patio to add a dash of color to a dull corner.

◆ GROWING TIPS ◆

Plant the bowl in early summer in cold areas, after the danger of frost has passed. To encourage healthy leaves, feed the display every two weeks with a low-nitrogen fertilizer. Remove flower spikes as they form so that the plant concentrates its energies on producing leaves.

BLOODLEAF
Iresine lindenii has leaf color that lasts through the summer until the first frosts. 10 plants.

Remove flowers as they appear to encourage healthy foliage.

Bulbous terracotta bowl, 4in (10cm) deep, 10in (25cm) wide.

Height
18in
(45cm)

Four o' Clocks

☼ SUN 🖌 MEDIUM-RICH POTTING MIX ☙ MOIST CONDITIONS

THIS TENDER PERENNIAL, which produces a potato-like tuber, needs a large pot to give its best. It forms mounds of bushy foliage with bright green leaves and a multitude of delicate flowerbuds in red, pink, yellow, white, or combinations. In this arrangement, there is a mix of carmine-pink and bright yellow blooms; seeds, however, are not sold by color so the flowers you get are down to chance. Place the pot close to a garden seat so you can enjoy the nocturnal flowers when they are open.

◆ Growing Tips ◆

Plant four o' clock seeds indoors in midspring for flowers in midsummer. When the chance of frost has passed, take the display into the garden. Feed once a week with a high-phosphorus fertilizer and water frequently during the flowering season. Like those of dahlia plants, the tubers can be stored through the winter until spring.

If this species is too large for your pot try 'Pygmaea,' a more compact plant. ●

● Four o' Clock
Mirabilis jalapa bears scented, trumpet-shaped flowers for three months. Two plants.

Flowers open during late afternoon, hence its name. ●

Height
34in
(85cm)

● *Terracotta pot, 16in (40cm) deep, 8in (20cm) wide.*

SALVIA SPIRES

☀ SUN/SEMISHADE ⚒ MEDIUM-RICH POTTING MIX ⚲ MOIST CONDITIONS

VIVID SCARLET SALVIA, *Salvia splendens*, is a half-hardy annual from Brazil, with vibrant, densely packed flower spikes that last throughout the summer months. On the whole, it requires very little maintenance. In this planting, a mixture of red, magenta-pink, and coral-pink salvias creates a striking clash of hot colors, which is heightened by the salvias' proximity to silvery plectostachys foliage. This is a rewarding planting for a sunny or semishaded paved area.

◆ GROWING TIPS ◆

Plant the salvias in early summer after the chance of frost has passed. Encourage healthy, bushy growth by pinching out the central growth point once. Remove dead flower spikes when the bracts turn brown.

PLECTOSTACHYS
Plectostachys serphyllifolia needs occasional trimming to keep the trails of foliage • *in check.* Three plants.

SALVIA
Salvia splendens 'Phoenix Mixed' flowers continuously until the first frosts. Five plants. •

Rub the silver leaves between your fingertips to release a • *fresh herby scent.*

Weathered terracotta pot; 16in (40cm) deep, • *8in (20cm) wide.*

Height
32in
(80cm)

AROMATIC APRICOT ROSES

☀ SUN/SEMISHADE 🍴 MEDIUM-RICH POTTING MIX ⚱ MOIST CONDITIONS

L OW-GROWING ROSES are best suited to container plantings; taller-growing varieties tend not to do so well in small spaces. This compact rose shrub, known as 'Sweet Magic Patio', has a continuous display of fragrant apricot-orange roses throughout summer and autumn. Planted with silvery blue-green lotus foliage, the roses appear vivid orange in contrast. The trailing habit of lotus also softens the hard edges of the lead tub. Place the planting next to a garden seat or on a path so you can enjoy the roses' delicious scent.

◆ GROWING TIPS ◆

Plant the roses in early spring, but introduce lotus at a later stage to avoid hard frost. Water the roses very occasionally in winter, and more regularly during the flowering season. The roses will grow well for a few years in a container this size before needing to be repotted.

ROSE
Rosa 'Sweet Magic Patio' must be deadheaded regularly to keep it looking its best through four months of nearly continuous ● flowering. Three plants.

LOTUS
Lotus berthelotii has feathery foliage and grows well in tubs.
● Four plants.

Antique lead tub; 16in (40cm) deep, ● 12in (30cm) wide.

In late summer, ● lotus foliage carries clusters of scarlet flowers.

Height
3ft
(1m)

PINK PHLOX WALL BASKET

☀ SEMISHADE   🛠 MEDIUM-RICH POTTING MIX   🧺 MOIST CONDITIONS

A STRETCH OF BLANK WALL on the side of the house or out-building in the garden can be brought to life with one or several basket plantings. This clever use of walls brings flowers and foliage to every area of the garden and is particularly useful when space is at a premium. Here, double pink phlox mixes with trailing helichrysum, plectranthus, and silver vine to produce a reliable, long-lasting display. Make sure that you can reach wall baskets to water them regularly, because they dry out quickly.

◆ GROWING TIPS ◆

Plant a selection of wall baskets in early summer. Water regularly and feed weekly with a high-nitrogen fertilizer to promote healthy foliage. Deadhead the phlox plants so that they continue to grow flowering stems. In autumn, replant silver vine into single pots and bring them indoors as houseplants.

PLECTRANTHUS
Plectranthus coleoides
'Variegatus' flourishes
in the confines of a wall
basket. Three plants.

PHLOX
Phlox paniculata 'Cherry Pink' is
easily grown and flowers profusely
in late summer. Two plants.

HELICHRYSUM
Helichrysum petiolare
'Variegatum' is a consistent
favorite with container
gardeners. One plant.

Terracotta wall basket,
14in (35cm) deep,
18in (45cm) wide.

Height
22in
(55cm)

SILVER VINE
Scindapsus pictus
'Argyraeus' can
be trained to climb up
a wall. Two plants.

MAGNIFICENT LILIES

☀ SUN/SEMISHADE   🖌 RICH POTTING MIX   ⚱ MOIST CONDITIONS

THE BEAUTY OF MANY LILIES is their trumpet-shaped flowers and sweet, spicy scent, which cannot be surpassed. Most types of lilies flower in midsummer; however, it is possible to have lilies in bloom for four months of the year since some flower in early summer and others not until autumn. Place several pots of scented lilies close to the patio where you sit outside, or under a window so that their perfume enters the house on summer evenings.

◆ **GROWING TIPS** ◆

Plant the lily bulbs in autumn or spring, depending on availability. As the bulbs grow, feed weekly. In winter, protect the plants from freezing. Repot every second year, taking care not to damage the roots.

LILY ◆
Lilium 'Troubador'
is a midsummer-
flowering hybrid,
derived from such
species as L. auratum
and L. speciosum.
10 bulbs.

Stake lily stems as soon as
the bulbs have been planted
to avoid damage. ◆

LILY ◆
Lilium 'Concorde'
is a hybrid derived
from such species as
L. lancifolium and
L. maculatum.
10 bulbs.

Painted wooden tub; ◆
12in (30cm) deep,
10in (25cm) wide.

Cut off dead flowers. ◆
Leave foliage stems since
they are needed to make
food for the following
year's growth.

Height
4ft
(1.2m)

LEAFY SELECTION

☀ SHADE/SEMISHADE   🖌 MEDIUM-RICH POTTING MIX   ⚗ MOIST CONDITIONS

A GLAZED STONEWARE TROUGH, brimming with the golden leaves of houttuynia, creeping Jenny, and pink and burgundy begonias, is a particularly lively combination that works very well because all the plants enjoy the same conditions. Gold variegated houttuynia thrives within the confines of a container, whereas in garden borders it is more difficult to use because it spreads rapidly and its leaf color seems at odds with the more subdued tones of other shade-loving plants. Position the trough against a wall in dappled shade. It can remain in this location throughout the summer months until the first frosts.

◆ GROWING TIPS ◆

Plant the trough in early summer, ensuring that there is good drainage. All the plants enjoy copious amounts of water. To encourage healthy, bushy foliage, feed twice monthly with a high-nitrogen fertilizer.

Height
20in
(50cm)

CREEPING JENNY
*Lysimachia nummularia
'Aurea' has leaves that
turn bright greenish yellow
● in shade.* Two plants.

HOUTTUYNIA
*Houttuynia cordata
'Heart of Gold'
bears foliage with a
distinctly tangy aroma.*
● Three plants.

BEGONIA
*Begonia semperflorens 'Flamingo' carries
a succession of pink-edged white flowers
for up to four months.* Two plants.

*Glazed stoneware trough;
8in (20cm) deep,
● 24in (60cm) long.*

AUTUMN

Clusters of fiery red and orange berries hanging on branches of pyracantha, cotoneaster, and viburnum provide container gardeners with a rich palette of autumnal color. The sun, although low in the sky, still makes its presence felt and brings on the last show of fuchsia, chrysanthemum, and gentian flowers. There is still time to enjoy the pleasure of being outside, and to plant bulbs, trees, and shrubs in pots for the year to come. Take some time to cherish the warmth of your autumn container displays in the glowing midday light.

❧❧

BERRY DISPLAY
Terracotta pots of pyracantha, low-spreading cotoneaster, and a standard elaeagnus stand against a sun-warmed wall in the golden autumn light. (See p.126 for details.)

FUCHSIA PLANTER

☀ SHADE/SEMISHADE 　🌱 MEDIUM-RICH POTTING MIX 　💧 MOIST CONDITIONS

T HERE ARE MANY varieties of fuchsias but they grow in a
limited range of colors from blue-pinks, shades of purple
and red, to whites. They are graceful shrubs and have an upright,
arching habit. Fuchsias are useful plants to remember when
planning container color because they flower heavily in cooler
spring weather and often produce a second wave of blooms in
autumn. A paved area at the top of a flight of steps makes a fine
setting in which to admire their pendulous flowers.

◆ GROWING TIPS ◆

Plant tender fuchsia shrubs after the
chance of frost has passed. Pinch out
a few of the growing tips so that the
plants become bushier; at first there
are fewer flowers, but in the long
term this pays dividends. Most
fuchsias cannot tolerate extreme
conditions of any kind, whether full
sun, heat, or freezing temperatures.

FUCHSIA
Fuchsia 'Cheviot Princess'
is a robust floriferous variety.
Four plants.

ENGLISH IVY
Hedera helix 'Eva',
*with its silvery green
and cream leaves,
trails around the edge
of the container.*
Four plants.

*Square plastic
Versailles planter;
15in (38cm) deep,
15in (38cm) wide.*

Height
30in
(75cm)

LEAFY TROUGH FOR SHADE

☀ SUN/SEMISHADE   🌡 MEDIUM-RICH POTTING MIX   ⚱ MOIST CONDITIONS

B OLD RED FLOWERS and dark green leaves make a truly vibrant contribution to this decorative terracotta trough, which should be brimming with flowers and foliage by early autumn. The juxtaposition of red and green makes both colors appear even brighter, and in a shady site the impatiens and clusters of begonia flowers really sing out. Position the planting along the edge of a patio wall to introduce a colorful focal point.

◆ GROWING TIPS ◆

Plant this trough in summer for autumn flowers. Pinch out the long flowering spires from the coleus plants to promote bushy foliage growth. Repot begonias before the first frosts, and overwinter inside.

BEGONIA
Begonia fuchsioides bears fuchsialike flowers in autumn and winter.
Three plants. ●

IMPATIENS
Impatiens Rosette Series can grow to a height of 24in (60cm).
Three plants. ●

Height
28in
(70cm)

SPIDER PLANT
Chlorophytum comosum 'Variegatum', *with its evergreen foliage, provides year-round interest.*
Two plants. ●

COLEUS
This coleus selection produces toothed, color-splashed leaves.
Two plants. ●

Pineapple-swagged terracotta trough; 7in (18cm) deep, 24in (60cm) long. ●

STARRY MARGUERITES

☀ SUN/SEMISHADE ⚱ MEDIUM-RICH POTTING MIX ⚜ MOIST CONDITIONS

ARGYRANTHEMUM 'PINK AUSTRALIAN', with its pink double flowers, is a hybrid marguerite which, until recently, was classified as a member of the Chrysanthemum genus. Although marguerites are not hardy, they are invaluable for container gardeners because they grow very quickly and produce an abundance of flowers throughout the summer and autumn months. Display this arrangement on a sunny but sheltered terrace to enjoy the daisylike flowers for months on end.

◆ GROWING TIPS ◆

Plant out after all chance of frost has passed, and remove leggy growths early on so that the plants grow into a sturdy mound. To encourage the optimum number of flowers, deadhead regularly. Overwinter marguerites indoors, or take cuttings to plant the following year.

Fresh green leaves are characteristic of this perennial.

Height
34in
(85cm)

Terracotta pot,
12in (30cm) deep,
8in (20cm) wide.

MARGUERITE
Argyranthemum frutescens
'Pink Australian' has
starburst petals with a
darker cushionlike center.
Three plants.

MICHAELMAS GLOW

☀ SUN/SEMISHADE   ⚒ MEDIUM-RICH POTTING MIX   ⚒ MOIST CONDITIONS

TWO VARIETIES OF HEUCHERA, both with dark evergreen leaves, form the core of this inspirational autumn planting: *Heuchera* 'Palace Purple' has plum-colored leaves, and *Heuchera* 'Pewter Moon' has pewter-colored leaves with maroon undersides. Here, delicate pink Michaelmas daisies are planted among the heuchera foliage and, by contrast, heighten its depth of color. Place this basket display on a paved patio area where it can be viewed from above for maximum impact.

◆ GROWING TIPS ◆

Plant the display in autumn or spring in a wire vegetable basket lined with moss and plastic to retain moisture. Cut several holes in the plastic lining to allow for drainage. To encourage the Michaelmas daisies to produce a good crop of flowers, feed the display every two weeks with a high-phosphorus fertilizer.

MICHAELMAS DAISY
Aster novi-belgii is fully hardy but often requires treatment against mildew.
Three plants. ●

HEUCHERA
Heuchera 'Palace Purple', *with its large purple leaves, provides rich color.*
● Two plants.

HEUCHERA ●
Heuchera 'Pewter Moon' *produces sprays of small white flowers in summer.* Two plants.

● *Wire vegetable basket, lined with moss and plastic; 8in (20cm) deep, 24in (60cm) wide.*

Height
18in
(45cm)

WAYS WITH WALLS

MEDITERRANEAN MIX (Left)
A selection of pots containing variegated yuccas and double red nasturtiums, plus bowls of succulents and impatiens, helps to disguise an uninspiring area of wall by introducing color and texture.

TUB OF TULIPS (Above)
An almost theatrical statement can be made in the smallest of outdoor spaces by standing a large terracotta pot packed with tulips in front of a salmon-pink wall. 'De Wet' tulips, with their magnificent colored flowers and delicious scent reminiscent of oranges, are excellent for this container planting. (See p.51 for details.)

AUTUMN COLOR (Left)
In autumn, a copper pot spilling over with osteospermum flowers and the rust-colored leaves of coleus captures the essence of the season. Here, both the copper container and the planting seem to complement the natural rustic red color of an old brick garden wall. (See p.127 for details.)

GENTIAN BLUE (Right)
The intense blue hue of autumn-flowering gentians, together with the pure white petals of cyclamen, creates a dramatic highlight in an oval-shaped terracotta trough sitting on an ivy-clad wall. (See p.125 for details.)

HEATHER HARMONY

☀ SUN/SEMISHADE 🪴 ACIDIC POTTING MIX 🛁 MOIST CONDITIONS

I N LATE SUMMER AND AUTUMN, caryopteris, the splendid shrub
with silvery aromatic leaves, produces tufts of misty blue-lilac
flowers. In this display, it is combined to harmonious effect with
an autumn-flowering pale pink heather, whose plumes of feathery
leaves contrast with trails of green-and-cream-variegated English
ivy. The square, weather-resistant ceramic container is glazed in
glowing deep red – a truly autumnal color – and looks fantastic
situated on a terrace.

• GROWING TIPS •
Plant the container in midspring.
Heather prefers an acidic potting
mix, whereas caryopteris and English
ivy grow well in any soil. Ensure the
potting mix is kept moist; heathers
do not like dry growing conditions.

CARYOPTERIS
Caryopteris x clandonensis
'Heavenly Blue'
flowers prolifically from
late summer to autumn.
Two plants. •

HEATHER
Calluna vulgaris
'Highland Spring'
has clear pink flowers
for up to two months.
• Four plants.

ENGLISH IVY
Hedera helix
'Sagittifolia
Variegata'.
Five plants. •

• *Glazed planter,*
11in (28cm) deep,
11in (28cm) wide.

Height
30in
(75cm)

AUTUMN GEMS

✳ SEMISHADE 🏺 LIME-FREE POTTING MIX 🖌 MOIST CONDITIONS

THE PURE BLUE COLOR of gentian flowers is one of the most intense pigments in the plant world. Although gentians are not the easiest plants to cultivate, containerized varieties have a better chance since you can control their growing conditions more closely. Autumn-flowering cyclamen, with its butterfly-like petals, enjoys a similar environment, so together they make an extremely happy pair. As an added bonus, this cyclamen has a deliciously sweet perfume. Make the most of the vivid blue of gentians by planting the display in a warm-colored terracotta pot, and place it in a sheltered site against a brick wall.

◆ **GROWING TIPS** ◆

Plant the container in summer in lime-free potting mix. Gentian and cyclamen are frost hardy but need a sheltered site, especially during cold winters. Every two or three years, remember to divide and repot all the plants during the spring months.

Height
12in
(30cm)

CYCLAMEN
Cyclamen cyprium, a tuberous-rooted plant, produces fragrant blooms from early autumn to
● *spring.* Three plants.

Cyclamen is found growing wild in woods and mountainous areas in
── *Mediterranean countries.*

GENTIAN
Gentiana sino-ornata 'Inverleith', like other Asiatic gentians, flowers in autumn, whereas European species flower throughout spring.
Two plants. ●

Ensure ●
that the soil is lime-free, or the leaves of this species will turn yellow.

● *Oval-shaped terracotta trough; 7in (16cm) deep, 14in (35cm) long.*

FIERY PYRACANTHAS

☀ SUN/SEMISHADE 🍴 MEDIUM-RICH POTTING MIX ⚖ MOIST CONDITIONS

PYRACANTHAS ARE VERY HANDSOME, strong-growing plants with needlelike thorns. For this reason, they are often grown as boundary hedges. Among their many attributes are their evergreen leaves, white clusters of hawthornlike flowers, and long-lasting red, orange, or yellow berries. In open ground, most pyracanthas grow into large shrubs, but they do very well in pots and can be trained by growing them on a trellis or pyramid. A sheltered site against a wall or fence is an ideal location for these attractive shrubs.

PYRACANTHA
Pyracantha rogersiana 'Golden Charmer' bears spires of white flowers in summer, which give way to vibrant orange-yellow berries.
One shrub. ●

PYRACANTHA ●
Pyracantha rogersiana 'Orange Charmer' has small evergreen leaves and glossy red-orange berries in autumn. One shrub.

Support the shrub as it ● grows with a trellis. (See p.150 for details.)

◆ GROWING TIPS ◆

Plant in pots in autumn or spring. Tie in shoots as necessary to maintain the shape of the shrubs, and cut back unwanted shoots as they appear. Bear in mind that heavy pruning will reduce the number of summer flowers and autumn berries. Pyracanthas are prone to diseases, such as fireblight and scab, but these two varieties are known for their natural resistance. Water freely in summer and feed every two weeks.

Terracotta pot; ● 12in (30cm) deep, 8in (20cm) wide.

Height
5ft
(1.5m)

AUTUMN DAISIES

☀ SUN   ⚗ MEDIUM-RICH POTTING MIX   ⬩ MOIST CONDITIONS

OSTEOSPERMUM IS A MEMBER of the daisy family. This variety has enchanting daisy flowers, with pale pink petals and dark purple eyes, which it produces in huge quantities in summer and autumn. Here, in a copper bowl, the aromatic silver-green leaves of osteospermum, interspersed with rust-colored coleus foliage, present a wonderful autumnal show. Both plants are perennial, but neither is hardy and so will not survive beyond the first autumn frosts. Place the bowl in a sheltered but sunny spot to keep the planting looking its best.

◆ GROWING TIPS ◆

Plant the pot in early summer. Feed once a week with a high-phosphorus fertilizer to encourage a mass of blooms in autumn. Deadhead the osteospermum flowers as they finish, and remove flower spikes and any straggly growth from the coleus plants to keep the arrangement looking bushy.

COLEUS
Coleus blumei is also known as flame nettle because of its brightly colored, nettlelike leaves. Two plants.

OSTEOSPERMUM
Osteospermum barberiae is a tender perennial that flowers for up to three months. Four plants.

Height
32in
(80cm)

*Weatherbeaten copper pot,
6in (15cm) deep,
10in (25cm) wide.*

CHEERY CHRYSANTHEMUMS

☀ SUN　🔧 MEDIUM-RICH POTTING MIX　⚱ MOIST CONDITIONS

CHRYSANTHEMUMS have bold rust, maroon, plum, orange, gold, or red flowers and are synonymous with autumn. Young plants can be easily purchased from garden centers and grown in pots. They are rewarding plants, producing a prolific display of blooms that last for several weeks. Chrysanthemums grow naturally to form a low mound of flowers, but they can be trained into pyramids or standards. Place several pots of red, orange, and yellow plants as a group on a paved area to bring vivid autumn color to your patio.

A single plant can produce hundreds of flowers in one season.

CUSHION CHRYSANTHEMUM
Chrysanthemum 'Zuki' is a dwarf plant that produces a multitude of star-shaped single flowers. One plant.

CUSHION CHRYSANTHEMUM •
Chrysanthemum 'Moonlight' has single daisylike flowers and a sweet tangy perfume. One plant.

◆ GROWING TIPS ◆

Plant chrysanthemums in a bright, sheltered position in early summer. Feed on a weekly basis with a high-phosphorus liquid fertilizer until the buds begin to show color in late summer. Remove long, straggly shoots to encourage bushy plants. Water frequently, but try not to saturate the soil.

SPRAY CHRYSANTHEMUM
This selection has long, tubular petals that form a spiky outline.
● Three plants.

● *Tall terracotta pot;
16in (40cm) deep,
6in (15cm) wide.*

● *Tall terracotta pot;
24in (60cm) deep,
6in (15cm) wide.*

Height
30in
(75cm)

WINTER

In winter, strong simple shapes, made by trees and shrubs without leaves, become elegant features in town and country gardens. Well-clipped topiary in plain glazed containers enhance this simple austerity, while other varieties of evergreens with pale green, silver, or gold foliage add a subtle beauty to displays. Indoors, the same pale beauty is offered by winter-flowering plants, such as jasmine and narcissus with their rich scents. For a flamboyant display of color, we need to turn to poinsettias, orchids, and other tropical plants to usher us through the winter months.

❧❦

CHEERY WINDOWBOX
A terracotta trough of evergreens can survive near-freezing temperatures. Here, Leucothoe 'Scarletta' has rich claret-colored leaves that mix beautifully with the brilliant red and orange berries of winter cherry. (See p. 142 for details.)

RED WINTER BERRIES

☼ SEMISHADE　🌡 ACIDIC POTTING MIX　🗲 MOIST CONDITIONS

I'VE ACHIEVED a cheery small-scale planting by growing winter-green, with its fat red berries and glossy leaves, and silvery blue juniper in a copper bowl. Both plants are quite hardy, which makes them an ideal choice for a winter planting. Wintergreens are often thought to be invasive plants and some, such as *Gaultheria shallon*, spread out over large areas by suckers. *Gaultheria procumbens*, used in this display, is not as invasive as other species and will grow quite happily for a couple of years within the confines of the container. Likewise, *Juniperus squamata* 'Blue Carpet' does well in containers; in the open it will spread farther to form a carpet of foliage up to 6ft (2m) wide. Place the copper bowl on the edge of a path to add interest to a winter display.

JUNIPER ●
Juniperus squamata 'Blue Carpet' *spreads out its branches of aromatic silvery blue foliage.* Two plants.

◆ GROWING TIPS ◆

In cold areas, plant the container in mid- to late spring to enable the wintergreens to establish themselves, since young plants can be damaged by frost. Handle juniper plants with gloves because they can cause a skin rash. Stand the pot in semishade away from trees dripping with rain-water, which wintergreens dislike. During summer, feed every two weeks with a high-phosphorus plant food to encourage a good crop of winter berries. Suitable for mild areas or with winter protection.

WINTERGREEN
*Gaultheria procumbens, with its
aromatic glossy green leaves, is
a fast-growing, creeping species
that can spread up to 3ft (1m)*
• *across. Two plants.*

*Leaves and fruit yield
wintergreen oil, which is*
• *used to flavor toothpaste.*

• *Aromatic red berries
follow white or pink
summer flowers during
winter months.*

• *Tarnished copper pot,
8in (22cm) deep,
12in (30cm) wide.*

Height
12in
(30cm)

MINTY EVERGREENS

☀ SUN/SEMISHADE 🥄 MEDIUM-RICH POTTING MIX ⚒ MOIST CONDITIONS

IT IS EASY TO ASSUME that all evergreens have dark, somber green foliage similar to laurel or yew. However, there are many with pale green, silver, or gold foliage that can add a luminous quality to winter arrangements. Here, gold-edged hebe leaves, silvery green-leaved senecio, gold and green euonymus, and cream-and-green-leaved English ivy grow in a white windowbox. All of these shrubs thrive in a container environment. To appreciate this low-maintenance display fully, place it on a window ledge with protection in cold winter areas.

• GROWING TIPS •

Plant in autumn or spring. Keep the arrangement well watered through the summer; water sparingly during warm winter spells, but not at all in freezing conditions. Suitable for mild areas or with winter protection.

Height
34in
(85cm)

HEBE
Hebe elliptica 'Variegata' tolerates atmospheric pollution and salty winds. One plant.

SENECIO
Senecio 'Sunshine' has leaves coated in a silvery felt which are soft to touch. Two plants.

EUONYMUS
Euonymus fortunei 'Emerald and Gold' has low-growing evergreen foliage and thrives in containers. One plant.

ENGLISH IVY
Hedera helix will grow in almost any potting mix or exposure. Five plants.

Weatherboard windowbox; 18in (45cm) deep, 34in (85cm) wide.

CHRISTMAS BASKET

☀ BRIGHT SHADE ⚱ MEDIUM-RICH POTTING MIX ⬦ DRY CONDITIONS

DURING WINTER, indoor container plantings come into their own, and this spectacular rustic basket, packed with pink-striped cyclamen and stippled gold-leaved piggyback plant, is no exception. Many indoor-flowering plants, such as cyclamen, find it difficult to survive in centrally heated rooms at this time of year. To prolong the life of this display, make sure you buy the cyclamen plants in peak condition, place the basket in a cool, draft-free site on a bright window ledge, and keep it moist.

♦ **GROWING TIPS** ♦

In autumn, plant cyclamens for indoor flowering in pots, with the top half of their tubers just above soil level. To delay flowering until Christmas, remove the first cyclamen buds. Water the display sparingly at the base of the piggyback plant.

• CYCLAMEN
Cyclamen persicum
'Giganteum' has flowers
that last longer if a steady
temperature of 55°F (12°C)
is maintained. Two plants.

PIGGYBACK PLANT
Tolmiea menzeisii
produces baby plants
on top of the larger
leaves, weighing them
down so that they
droop over the sides.
• Two plants.

Heart-shaped
leaves are blotched
with silver. •

Rustic wicker basket;
6in (16cm) deep,
22in (55cm) wide. •

Height
18in
(45cm)

TRADITIONAL TOPIARY

☀ SUN/BRIGHT SHADE   🛠 MEDIUM-RICH POTTING MIX   🕏 MOIST CONDITIONS

T HE GREAT JOY OF TOPIARY is that it looks fantastic throughout the year, but it comes into its own in winter when well-clipped evergreens in simple geometric shapes, such as cones, cubes, pyramids, and domes, give the often bare garden an architectural formality. Boxwood and yew, in particular, and shrubs with tight-knit foliage, such as bay, can be trained or clipped into almost any form, and require the minimum of maintenance outside the growing season. Plant topiary trees in frost-proof pots to bring interest to patios through the year.

Sweet bay is one of the few laurels that is not poisonous.

SWEET BAY •
Laurus nobilis is not the hardiest of shrubs and grows best in a sheltered site; young leaves can be easily damaged by cold winds. One tree.

Aromatic, evergreen • leaves. Bay plants are traditionally trimmed into rounded shapes.

• GROWING TIPS •
Plant the ceramic pots in autumn or spring. For healthy foliage, feed monthly during the growing season with a nitrogen-rich fertilizer. Trim all the topiary trees into shape two or three times during the growing season; do the last trimming a month before the first expected autumn frost. In warm winter spells, water the bay tree to keep the potting mix just moist. Boxwood trees need less frequent watering. Suitable for mild areas or with winter protection.

Large glazed pot; 20in (50cm) deep, 30in (75cm) wide.

COMMON BOXWOOD
Buxus sempervirens, although slow-growing, is a traditional choice for topiary in pots. Clip regularly to maintain its shape. One tree per pot. •

With its densely packed • *foliage, common boxwood was a favorite topiary plant in Roman times.*

Overwinter potted topiary indoors in areas with below-freezing weather. •

• *Jade-green glazed pot; 15in (38cm) deep, 20in (50cm) wide.*

Height
3ft
(1m)

CONTAINERS IN CONSERVATORIES

FRAGRANT FLOWERS (*Left*)
Before the first frosts, bring individual pots of jasmine and narcissus into a warm, light-filled conservatory or garden room. They will produce a succession of flowers throughout the winter months, filling the room with their deliciously sweet scent. (*See* *p.140 for details.*)

EXOTIC GARDEN ROOM (*Below*)
Sophisticated-looking plants, such as these cymbidium orchids and crimson azaleas, enjoy the cool but sheltered environment of a bright garden room through the winter. They will both flower prolifically into the following spring, when they can be placed outdoors in their containers.

ARMCHAIR COMPANIONS (*Above*)
Bring summer into a semishady area of a conservatory by planting individual pots of regal geraniums and frothy white hydrangeas. Maidenhair ferns also look attractive, forming an umbrella of cool green foliage.

INDOOR HANGING BASKET (*Below*)
A mass of deep pink bell-shaped flowers of Kalanchoe 'Wendy' looks fantastic spilling over the edges of a late-winter hanging basket in a sheltered conservatory room.

FRAGRANT WHITES

✹ BRIGHT SHADE 🌡 MEDIUM-RICH POTTING MIX ⚱ MOIST CONDITIONS

JASMINE AND PAPERWHITE NARCISSUS both carry pure white flowers with a deliciously sweet fragrance, making them an attractive winter container pairing. *Jasminum polyanthum* is a half-hardy climbing species, whose branching stems are bursting with clouds of starlike flowers by midwinter. Paperwhite narcissus produce a succession of flowers from early winter until midspring if planted every few weeks. Both plants are frost tender and need to be grown indoors; their fragrance is so magnificent that no conservatory should be without them.

◆ GROWING TIPS ◆

In summer and early autumn, plant jasmine in pots outdoors; feed twice monthly with a high-phosphorus food. Bring indoors before first frost and keep cool. During the flowering season, water freely and deadhead regularly. Plant narcissus bulbs in bulb fiber or loose soil mix six weeks before you want them to bloom. Keep the soil moist; store in a dark room until shoots appear, then place in a bright but sheltered situation.

● JASMINE
Jasminum polyanthum is thought to flower best when its stems are trained horizontally, so try growing the plant around a wire hoop or over a bamboo trellis. One plant.

● PAPERWHITE NARCISSUS
Narcissus 'Paperwhite Grandiflora' has about eight flowers to a stem. Stake the stems to keep them upright. 15 bulbs.

Moss-and-plastic-lined wire wastepaper basket; 12in (30cm) deep, ● 10in (25cm) wide.

Green metal bucket; 10in (25cm) deep ● 8in (20cm) wide.

Height
3ft
(1m)

BUDDING SKIMMIAS

☼ SEMISHADE ⚱ RICH POTTING MIX ⚘ MOIST CONDITIONS

SKIMMIAS ARE APPEALING SHRUBS for winter plantings since they bear aromatic evergreen leaves and decorative clusters of flowerbuds that stay intact until spring. Viburnum also carries flowerbuds in winter, though they may burst into flower during spells of mild weather. The final ingredient is gold-variegated English ivy, whose trailing leaves look sunny all year. Plant this mix in a clay urn to make an attractive focal point for a patio or terrace, and position it where it can be seen from a haven of warmth inside your home.

◆ GROWING TIPS ◆

Plant in autumn or spring. During the growing season feed monthly with a high-phosphorus fertilizer. This planting can remain in the same container for a few years; even when it is not in flower, the foliage will continue to look fresh and attractive for the rest of the year. Suitable for mild areas or with winter protection.

SKIMMIA
Skimmia japonica 'Rubella' may suffer damage to young leaves during severe frost. Two plants.

VIBURNUM •
Viburnum tinus 'Eve Price' produces bright pink buds that open out into pale pink flowers. One plant.

SKIMMIA •
Skimmia laureola has cream flowerbuds and, like other skimmias, can tolerate atmospheric pollution. Two plants.

ENGLISH IVY
Hedera helix 'Harald' has evergreen leaves with bright gold edges. Four plants. •

Height
32in
(80cm)

• *Smooth clay urn, 12in (30cm) deep, 20in (50cm) wide.*

WINTER CHERRIES

☀ SUN/SEMISHADE   🖌 ACIDIC POTTING MIX   🥄 DRY CONDITIONS

FOR THOSE WHO LIVE in milder climates, there are a number of attractive plants that can be added to the outdoor palette and which, although not hardy, will survive the winter weather if placed in a sheltered site. Winter cherry, with its shiny orange berries, is a colorful choice – as are azaleas. Here, I've planted winter cherry with the maroon and green leaves of leucothoe and a swath of trailing English ivy. Place the trough against a wall or on a windowsill to shelter it from harsh elements.

◆ GROWING TIPS ◆

Plant the trough in autumn. As long as the temperature does not drop below 45°F (7°C), the winter cherry, leucothoe, and ivy will last for two years. Keep the soil almost dry, and withhold water in freezing conditions. Feed twice monthly.

Height
24in
(60cm)

ENGLISH IVY
Hedera helix 'Glacier'
trails down to break up
the horizontal thrust of
the winter display.
● Five plants.

LEUCOTHOE
Leucothoe fontanesiana 'Scarletta'
carries attractive evergreen foliage
throughout the year.
Two plants. ●

WINTER CHERRY
Solanum pseudocapsicum has star-
shaped white flowers in summer,
followed by scarlet fruit in winter.
Three plants. ●

● *Swag-motif*
terracotta trough;
10in (25cm) deep,
20in (50cm) wide.

RUSTIC INDOOR BASKET

☀ BRIGHT SHADE   🌱 MEDIUM-RICH POTTING MIX   ⚱ MOIST CONDITIONS

THE WINTER HOLIDAYS are the time to bring decorative
container plantings indoors. Here, pale pink azaleas are
planted with soft pink-and-cream-colored poinsettias and bright
scarlet and yellow primulas. All three plants enjoy similar growing
conditions and are readily available at garden centers. Place this
rustic basket on a bright window ledge away from radiators; the
cooler the room, the longer the arrangement will last.

◆ GROWING TIPS ◆

Plant the basket in late autumn, and
remember to cut drainage holes in
the plastic lining. Choose plants
with plenty of buds that are just
coming into flower. The azalea
likes to be well watered: do not
allow its fibrous roots to dry out.

POINSETTIA
Euphorbia pulcherrima 'Peaches and
Cream' *produces a poisonous milky
white sap, so wash your hands after
handling this plant.* One plant.

AZALEA
Rhododendron 'Pink Pearl'
*is an evergreen hybrid that
carries soft pink flowers until
spring.* One plant.

*Azaleas like more water than
the other plants in the basket,
so water the display liberally
from the righthand side.*

PRIMULA
*Many primulas are suitable
for containers, although they
are chiefly grown outdoors.*
Three plants.

*Plastic-lined
twig basket;
6in (15cm) deep,
14in (35cm) wide.*

Height
18in
(45cm)

PLANT CARE

*E*quip yourself with a few basic tools, such as a hand trowel and a watering can, and follow the simple procedures outlined on these pages to establish the best growing and flowering conditions for your plants. Techniques for preparing containers and then potting the different types of plant in tubs, windowboxes, and hanging baskets are carefully explained. Practical advice is given on how to maintain a long-lasting display, and there is also information on repotting plants, supporting stems, and training shrubs.

❧❧

STARTING FROM SCRATCH
Choose a suitable container from the enormous range now available, then purchase your plants, potting mix, and trowel. You are now ready to try your hand at container gardening.

PREPARING CONTAINERS

With all containers, whether made of stone, terracotta, ceramic, concrete, or wood, it is a good idea to remove leftover soil from the pots and scrub out the inside with disinfectant. By following these simple procedures you will prevent pests and diseases, which might be present on the container's surface, infesting and infecting your healthy plants, and therefore give them the best possible start for a long-lasting display.

1 Using a stiff brush, scrub out the inside of the container with disinfectant solution to kill bacteria and fungal spores.

2 Cover the drainage hole with flowerpot pieces, concave-side down, to help water find its way of escaping.

CLEAN START
To disinfect porous containers and the broken pieces of clay flowerpot that your are using to aid drainage, you will need disinfectant solution, a stiff scrubbing brush, and a large bucket of clean water with which to rinse out the inside of the container thoroughly.

POTTING MIXES
When planting containers, buy bags of ready-made neutral, acidic, or alkaline potting mix at the garden center. Add compost to enrich the mix, peat moss to improve the texture, and sand and gravel to promote good drainage.

PEAT MOSS

POTTING MIX

COMPOST

GRAVEL

SAND

SHRUB PLANTING

Careful planting will determine whether a plant flourishes and is long-lasting, or wilts and has a shortened lifespan. Once you have cleaned out the container, and placed several broken pot pieces over the drainage hole, fill the pot with the appropriate potting mix. If the container is large, it is best to fill it layer by layer, firming gently with your fingertips. This avoids compacting the soil, which would inhibit drainage.

SELECTING PLANTS
Choose plants with compact, healthy foliage and a good strong root system. Avoid plants with sparse stems and densely packed roots.

1 Fill the pot three-quarters full with soil, and press in the plant's original pot to establish how much space the shrub needs.

2 Loosen the tightly packed soil and root ball and, holding the shrub firmly at the base of the stem, lower it into the container.

3 Firm new soil around the sides of the root ball, building up the soil until it reaches the same level as the soil around the shrub.

4 Water the shrub thoroughly after planting. Remember that porous terracotta pots soak up moisture especially quickly.

CONDITIONING PLANTS

Before planting, dip the plant in its pot into a bucket of cold water. Hold the pot and plant just below water level for a few seconds, until all air bubbles are released from the potting mix, and it is thoroughly moist.

WINDOWBOX PLANTING

Prepare the windowbox (*see p.146*) and, before you begin planting, place it *in situ*, partly filled with moistened potting mix since it will be too heavy to lift onto a window ledge when it is packed with plants and watered. Always plant as generously as possible so that flowers and foliage spill over the edges as they grow. Leave space for fast-growing plants to expand, but bring slow-growers close together. When complete, give all the plants a thorough watering and feed them regularly as they grow to keep them healthy. When the flowers are past their best, dig out the plants (*see p.153*) and replace with another selection.

1 Before planting, work out where you want to place each plant and how many you need. I usually place tall plants toward the back of the box, and trailing plants along the front and sides.

2 Lift each plant out of its pot by placing your fingers across the base of the stem and turning the pot upside down; tap the pot on a hard edge and extract the plant. Gently loosen the roots.

3 Continue planting, working from right to left, firming the soil with your fingertips around each plant as you go. Fill in the sides of the container with some potting mix to just below the rim.

PLANTING BULBS

For a striking show of flowers, grow plenty of bulbs in each pot. The planting depth depends on the bulb size. As a general rule, plant each bulb at a depth equal to twice its own depth.

1 Using your fingertips, set the bulbs firmly in the pot, allowing a little space between each one.

2 Cover the bulbs in potting mix, up to 1in (2.5cm) below the container rim. Firm gently.

LAYERS OF BULBS
To make the most of available space, plant layers of different bulbs in one container. These will then flower at different times during the season. Here I've planted early flowering crocuses just below the surface, with later-flowering tulips somewhat deeper in the container.

HANGING BASKET PLANTING

I usually overplant hanging baskets because they look most spectacular when overflowing with flowers and have plenty of trailing foliage. A hanging basket has a rounded base, so it is a good idea to stand it in a plastic pot when planting to keep it steady and prevent it from toppling over. Ensure that the basket sits high on the pot so that plants can be threaded into the sides of the display.

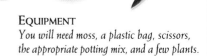

EQUIPMENT
You will need moss, a plastic bag, scissors, the appropriate potting mix, and a few plants.

1 Balance the basket on a pot, uncouple the chains, and line the interior with sphagnum moss.

2 Next, insert a plastic bag and pierce with scissors for good drainage. Add some potting mix.

3 Prepare the plants you wish to thread through the sides of the basket by wrapping in plastic.

4 Using scissors, make several long slits in the basket's plastic lining. Working from the inside to the outside, thread through each wrapped plant.

5 Slide the plastic off each plant, and gently pack moist potting mix around the roots. Begin filling out the main body of the display with flowering plants.

6 Place larger plants toward the middle and trailing plants at the sides, building up the level of potting mix as you go. Hang the basket *in situ* before watering.

STAKING AND TRAINING

Staking is one of the best ways to provide support for the stems of free-standing plants in large containers, especially those situated in exposed sites. Tall perennials and annuals require only single stakes, while climbers, shrubs, and trees may need a sturdier tripod of stakes or a trellis. Some small trees and shrubs can be trained to create a variety of interesting plant shapes.

DISCIPLINED PYRACANTHAS
Here, two pyracantha shrubs are staked in different ways: one is trained on a bamboo trellis to grow flush against a wall; the other is supported by a wigwam of bamboo stakes and is free-standing.

• Check how high the shrub is likely to grow to ensure that the stakes are long enough from the outset.

Tie the top • of the trellis to a wall to keep it steady.

Choose a • heavy, frost-proof terracotta or stone pot; shallow pots are not suitable for staked plants.

• Bury the legs of the trellis in the potting mix before planting to avoid damaging the shrub's roots.

CONSTRUCTING A BAMBOO TRELLIS

To make a gently widening trellis, you will need four 5ft- (1.5m-) long bamboo stakes and nine 14in- (35cm-) long stakes, garden wire, a pair of pliers, and pruners. Lay the shorter stakes across the longer ones, and tie them together with garden wire as described below.

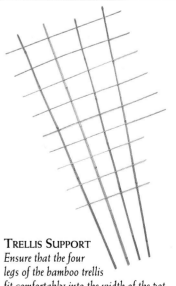

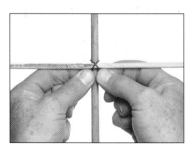

1 Position one vertical and then one horizontal piece of bamboo stake at right angles, and bind them togther around the point where they join in an X-shape with wire.

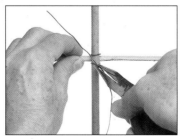

2 Use a pair of pliers to tighten the binding on the reverse side. Attach the bottom and top rung and then evenly space the other seven stakes between the two.

TRELLIS SUPPORT
Ensure that the four legs of the bamboo trellis fit comfortably into the width of the pot before you start to bind the trellis stakes together with garden wire or string.

TRAINING A STANDARD FUCHSIA

1 At a height of about 6in (15cm), remove all the sideshoots to promote rapid upward growth.

2 As the plant grows, continue to remove sideshoots, and tie the main stem to a bamboo stake.

3 At 3ft (1m) tall, allow three more sets of leaves to form, then pinch out the growing tip.

4 At 6in (15cm) long, pinch out the tips of the sideshoots so that they will branch once more.

STANDARD FUCHSIA
Feed with a nitrogen-rich fertilizer twice weekly until the stem has grown, then use a phosphorus-rich fertilizer three times a week.

CLIPPING AND SHAPING TOPIARY TREES

1 Using pruners, trim the young boxwood plant into a cone shape, making sure that you do not cut the main growing tip.

2 At a height of 3ft (1m), use shears to trim the tree into a cone shape. Lean a stake against the sides to act as a cutting guide.

3 Maintain the cone shape of the mature boxwood tree by trimming the tree at least twice a year, during spring and summer.

PLANT MAINTENANCE

Plants grown in containers are quite simple to look after if you water, feed, and deadhead them as recommended in the *Growing Tips* that accompany all the planting projects. As a general rule, try to use a high-phosphorus liquid fertilizer during the growing season to produce the maximum number of flowers, and a high-nitrogen fertilizer to ensure healthy and bushy foliage growth.

DEADHEADING

Cut off dead blooms at the stem joint to prolong the flowering season; leave them on the plant if you want berries or seedheads.

TOP-DRESSING

1 Most shrubs can grow in the same pot for a few years if they are nourished with compost. First, scrape off about 2in (5cm) of soil.

2 Using a trowel, replace this top layer of soil with some fresh compost mixed with a slow-release fertilizer, then water well.

REPOTTING SPRING BULBS

Bulbs, especially narcissi, do not like to be overcrowded. It is best to repot them each year, in autumn; otherwise they will not flower well and will produce undersized or unhealthy foliage. When you are repotting, remove any rotting or dead bulb material to maintain a healthy planting.

1 Turn out the contents of the pot and carefully pick out the bulbs, discarding any damaged ones.

2 Separate out clumps of bulbs by gently pulling them apart, and remove loose outer layers.

REPLANTED BULBS (*Above*)
Carefully dust the bulbs with a fungicide and plant in moist potting mix (see p.148).

REPLANTING

By the end of summer, the flowering annuals
in hanging baskets are often past their best,
though foliage plants, such as ivies, remain
healthy and can be retained in the display as
the foundation for the next season's planting.

REPLANTING A HANGING BASKET

1 Using a hand trowel, carefully
dig out all the spent summer-
flowering annuals. Loosen the soil
and fill in with fresh if necessary.

2 Plant a selection of evergreens
or winter-flowering plants in
their place. Firm the soil and then
water the basket thoroughly.

REJUVENATED PLANTING
*Plants such as skimmias and heathers will
thrive in mild winters if they are planted in
an acidic-based potting mix.*

REPOTTING A TIRED-LOOKING SHRUB

1 Repot a shrub if its leaves are
wilting and if it lacks vitality.
First, ease out the shrub from its
pot and loosen the root ball.

2 Place broken pots and potting
mix in the bottom of the new
pot, which should be about 2in
(5cm) wider than the old one.

3 Center the plant and fill in
with potting mix, firming as
you go until the soil level is the
same as in the previous pot.

PLANT LIST

TREES AND SHRUBS

Abutilon x hybridum
(Abutilon)
Frost-tender, evergreen shrub.
Varieties carry red, pink, and
yellow bell-shaped, pendent
flowers throughout summer and
autumn months. Plant in sun in
well-drained, medium-rich potting
mix, and keep well watered.

Argyranthemum
(Marguerite)
Frost-tender, evergreen shrub.
Several species produced many
cultivars with profusion of single
and double daisy flowers in red,
pink, yellow, and white in summer
and autumn. Grow in sun in well-
drained, medium-rich potting mix,
and feed weekly in summer.

Artemisia 'Silver Brocade'
(Artemisia)
Frost-hardy, evergreen, spreading
sub-shrub with silvery aromatic
leaves and yellow flowers in
summer. Plant in sunny site in
medium-rich potting mix.

Buxus sempervirens
(Common Boxwood)
Frost-hardy, evergreen shrub or
tree. Grow in sun or bright shade
in medium-rich potting mix. Feed
monthly in growing season.

Calluna vulgaris
(Heather)
Frost-hardy, evergreen shrub. Grow
in sun or semishady sites in acidic
potting mix. Feed once a week in
summer and autumn months, and
water well with rainwater.

Camellia japonica
(Camellia)
Evergreen shrub producing single
and double flowers in red, pink,
cream, and white in spring. Protect
from early morning sun and grow
in semishade in well-drained,
acidic potting mix.

Caryopteris clandonensis
(Caryopteris)
Medium-sized deciduous shrub
with aromatic silver leaves and
whorls of feathery blue flowers in
late summer and autumn. Grow in
sun or semishade in well-drained,
medium-rich potting mix.

Euonymus fortunei
(Euonymus)
Evergreen shrub with attractive
leaves. Well-suited to pot culture.
Plant in medium-rich potting mix
in sun or semishade. Water well
in growing season.

Euphorbia pulcherrima
(Poinsettia)
Part of large genus of both
temperate and tropical shrubs.
Often grown as indoor plant for
Christmas market. Keep out of
drafts and ensure that potting
mix is kept moist.

Fuchsia
Half-hardy evergreen shrubs that
are deciduous in cooler regions.
Large number of flowering types
available but in a limited range of
colours. Late summer and autumn
months are the best flowering
seasons. Grow in well-drained,
medium-rich or rich potting mix,
in semishaded site. Feed and water
well during growing season.

Gaultheria procumbens
(Wintergreen)
Evergreen, spreading sub-shrub
with small, glossy green leaves
turning red in winter. White
flowers followed by scarlet berries
in autumn and winter. Grow in
shade or semishade in well-
drained, acidic potting mix. Keep
plants well watered throughout
growing season.

Hebe
Genus of half-hardy evergreen
shrubs with flowers in pinks,
purples, and whites. Variegated-
leaved hebes, such as H. elliptica,
are useful for winter container
plantings in sheltered sites. Plant
in sun or semishade in well-
drained, medium-rich potting mix.

Hedera
(English Ivy)
Evergreen climbers and trailers
that are ideal for pot culture, both
as secondary and main features in
plantings. Leaves vary from rich
green through gold, silver, and
cream variegations. Grow in any
exposure in well-drained, medium-
rich, preferably alkaline, potting
mix. Keep well watered through
growing season.

Helichrysum petiolare
(Helichrysum)
Trailing, evergreen shrub grown
as annual for its foliage. Varieties
have silver, gold, and variegated
leaves. Grow in any well-drained
potting mix. Helichrysum petiolare is
excellent for hanging baskets, or
plant to trail over edges in troughs,
sinks, tubs, and pots.

Hydrangea macrophylla
(Hydrangea)
Deciduous shrub with mop-
headed flowers in red, pink,
white, and blue. Grow in semishade in acidic potting mix, and
water well in growing season.

Jasminum polyanthum
(Jasmine)
Frost-tender evergreen climber
producing fragrant white flowers
in winter. Grow indoors in cool
garden room or conservatory in
medium-rich potting mix. Keep
well watered; feed twice monthly
with high-phosphorus fertilizer.

Juniperus squamata
(Juniper)
Evergreen, spreading conifer with
intense silvery blue leaves. Grow
in sun or semishade in well-
drained, medium-rich potting
mix. Water sparingly.

Lantana camara
(Lantana)
Frost-tender evergreen shrub with
long succession of flowers.
Cultivars available in hot pink,
red, orange, yellow, and white.
Grow in sun in rich potting mix.

Laurus nobilis
(Bay)
Evergreen tree, usually grown in
container as clipped shrub. Grow
in sun or semishade in well-
drained, rich potting mix. Keep
just moist and water throughout
winter, except when temperature
falls below freezing. Overwinter
indoors in cold areas.

Leucothöe fontanesiana
(Leucothöe)
Evergreen shrub with white bell-
shaped flowers in spring. Several
varieties have colorful leaves.
Grow in well-drained, acidic
potting mix, in sheltered site
in shade or semishade.

Plectostachys serphyllifolia
(Plectostachys)
Frost-tender, evergreen shrub
with small trailing silvery leaves.
Grow in well-drained, medium-
rich potting mix in sunny or
semishaded position. Plectostachys
looks particularly attractive in
hanging baskets and trailing over
edges of pots and tubs.

Prunus
(Cherry)
Deciduous trees with double pink
blossoms in spring. Cut back stems
after flowering to encourage new
flowers for following season. Plant
in well-drained, medium-rich
potting mix in sunny sites.

Pyracantha
(Pyracantha)
Evergreen shrub with white
flowers in summer followed by
red, orange, and yellow berries.
Plant in sun or semishade in well-
drained, medium-rich potting mix.
Keep well watered in summer. If
necessary, support this tall-
growing shrub with stakes.

Rhododendron
(Rhododendron and Azalea)
Evergreen and deciduous shrubs
and trees with showy flowers in
all colors but true blue. Grow all
species in acidic potting mix in
semishade, sheltered from cold
winds. Azaleas are generally
small-leaved and dwarf shrubs
with profuse blooms.

Rosa
(Rose)
Hardy, shorter varieties are most
suitable for containers. Grow in
sunny or semishaded position in
well-drained, medium-rich potting
mix. Water well during growing
season and feed weekly.

Scindapsus pictus
(Silver Vine)
Frost-tender, evergreen shrub with
climbing or trailing habit. Plant
outdoors in summer containers.
Grows particularly well in quite
sheltered, semishady sites in well-
drained, medium-rich potting mix.

Senecio maritima
(Senecio)
Frost-tender, evergreen sub-shrub grown for its feathery silver leaves. Enjoys sunny position in well-drained, medium-rich potting mix. (See also Succulents.)

Skimmia
Evergreen shrubs carrying attractive clusters of flowerbuds in autumn, often in conjunction with berries. Sweet-scented flowers open in spring. Grow in semishade in well-drained rich potting mix. Water well.

Solanum pseudocapsicum
(Winter Cherry)
Half-hardy evergreen shrub grown for its red, orange, white, and yellow berries. Grow in sheltered location in sunny site in well-drained, medium-rich potting mix.

Syringa meyeri
(Miniature Lilac)
Low-growing, deciduous shrub with small, sweet-scented lilac-pink flowers in late spring and early summer. Grow in sun in alkaline-rich potting mix.

Thymus
(Thyme)
Evergreen, mat-forming and dome-shaped sub-shrubs. Plant in sunny location in well-drained, medium-rich potting mix.

Viburnum tinus
(Viburnum)
Evergreen shrub with clusters of white-flushed pink flowers during winter and spring. Grow in well-drained, medium-rich potting mix in sun or semishade.

BAMBOO AND FERNS

Adiantum
(Maidenhair Fern)
Frost-tender ferns with delicate feathery green fronds. Plant in rich potting mix and site in sheltered position in semishade.

Pogonathemum paniceum
(Bamboo Grass)
Frost-tender, miniature bamboo grass with distinctive pink leaf tips. Grow in bright semishade in medium-rich potting mix.

Polypodium vulgare
(Creeping Fern)
Evergreen creeping fern with lacy fronds. Grow in shade or semi-shade in well-drained, medium-rich potting mix. Most ferns thrive in a damp environment.

Polystichum aculeatum
(Hard Shield Fern)
Evergreen or semi-evergreen fern with bright green fronds. Grow in semishade or shade in well-drained rich potting mix, and keep planting moist.

PERENNIALS

Ajuga reptans
(Ajuga/Bugle)
Evergreen, spreading perennial with deep purple leaves and spikes of intense blue-violet flowers in spring. Plant in medium-rich potting mix and grow in either sunny or shady site.

Aster novi-belgii
(Michaelmas Daisy)
Autumn-flowering hardy perennial with daisy flowers in red, pink, violet, purple, and white. Grow in sun or bright shade in well-drained, medium-rich potting mix.

Begonia
Genus divided into several groups, including Semperflorens (half-hardy annuals) and Tuberous (annuals). Tender evergreens producing masses of flowers in all colors except blue throughout summer and autumn. Grow in shade or semishade in medium-rich potting mix. Feed weekly. Propagate by seed, stem cuttings, or division of tubers.

Campanula poscharskyana
(Campanula)
Evergreen, spreading hardy perennial with lilac flowers in summer. Grow in medium-rich soil in sun or semishade.

Chlorophytum comosum
(Spider Plant)
Frost-tender, evergreen perennial with fountain of thin variegated leaves. Useful for outdoor summer plantings and as houseplant. Grow in medium-rich potting mix in semishade or shade.

Chrysanthemum (Dendranthemum)
Genus of perennials and annuals with daisylike flowers in many colors. Cushion chrysanthemums flower in autumn and are good for pot culture. Grow in medium-rich potting mix in sun or semishade.

Convolvulus sabatius
(Convolvulus)
Perennial with trailing habit. Host of purple-blue trumpet-shaped flowers in summer and autumn months. Grow in sunny location in sheltered site in well-drained, medium-rich potting mix.

Cymbalaria muralis
(Ivy-leaved Toadflax)
Creeping hardy perennial with ivy-shaped leaves and tiny purple flowers. Good in containers as underplanting for taller shrubs. Grow in any potting mix.

Erigeron
Perennials producing masses of pink, purple, and lilac daisylike flowers throughout summer. Grow in sun in medium-rich potting mix. Feed twice monthly.

Gaillardia x grandiflora
(Blanket Flower)
Perennial with long succession of orange and yellow daisy flowers in summer. Grow in well-drained, medium-rich potting mix in sunny position. Keep well watered and feed once a week.

Gentiana sino-ornata
(Gentian)
Frost-hardy, spreading, evergreen perennial with true blue flowers in autumn. Grow in sheltered position, in sun or semishade, in acidic potting mix. Keep well-watered in growing season.

Heuchera
Frost-hardy, evergreen perennial with rosettes of leaves in green, purple, and silver. Grow in shade or semishade in medium-rich potting mix. Water well.

Houttuynia cordata
(Houttuynia)
Vigorous perennial with pink-, cream-, and gold-variegated leaves. Grow in semishady sites and keep well watered.

Iresine lindenii
(Blood Leaf)
Frost-tender perennial grown for its colorful leaves. Remove flower spikes as they appear, to encourage healthy foliage. Grow in medium-rich potting mix, in bright light to retain leaf color.

Lysimachia nummularia
(Lysimachia)
Golden-leaved, trailing perennial with buttercup-like flowers in summer. Grow in sun or semi-shade in medium-rich potting mix in hanging baskets.

Mirabilis jalapa
(Four o' Clock)
Tuberous perennial with scented flowers in red, pink, white, and yellow, from midsummer until autumn. Remove tubers from soil in autumn and store indoors over winter months.

Origanum onites
(Pot Marjoram)
Aromatic herb grown in pots or as houseplant. Grow in sun in well-drained, medium-rich potting mix.

Origanum vulgare
(Oregano)
Frost-hardy, aromatic herb whose delicate, spicy flavor is used for cooking. Grow in sunny site in well-drained, medium-rich alkaline potting mix. Cut back old plant stems during spring.

Osteospermum
Short-lived evergreen perennials usually grown as annuals. Species have flowers in pink, purple, white, and yellow, some with quilled petals. Grow in sun in well-drained, medium-rich potting mix for flowers in summer and autumn months.

Oxalis lobata
(Oxalis)
Fast-growing perennial with clover-like leaves and yellow flowers in summer and autumn. Grow in well-drained medium-rich potting mix in sunny position, and shelter in cold weather. Good for summer hanging baskets.

Paphiopedilum callosum
(Slipper Orchid)
Frost-tender, evergreen orchid with veined white flowers borne on tall, thin stems in spring and summer. Grow indoors in cool conservatory or garden room. Plant in bark chips or in orchid potting mix in semishade. Feed twice monthly.

Phalaenopsis equestris
(Epiphytic Orchid)
Frost-tender perennial with flamboyant flowers; best grown in orchid potting mix in bright shade in conservatory or garden room.

Plectranthus coleoides
(Plectranthus)
Frost-tender, trailing evergreen perennial often grown as annual, with wavy-edged variegated leaves. Grow in medium-rich potting mix in any site. Cut back straggly growth as necessary to keep foliage healthy and bushy.

Polygonum
Several species suitable for growing in containers available, particularly the well-known frost-tender P. 'Victory Carpet' with its clusters of pink flowers. Grow in medium-rich potting mix in any number of sites. Water well during growing season.

Primula
(Primrose)
Hardy to frost-tender. Many species, particularly *P. vulgaris* (common), *P. veris* (cowslip), *P. denticulata*, and *P. obconica*, make good container plants. Grow in semishady site in well-drained, rich potting mix. Water well.

Ranunculus asiaticus
(Persian Buttercup)
Summer-flowering half-hardy perennials with peony-like flowers in red, pink, yellow, and white, early in season. Grow in sheltered position in sunny or semishaded position in well-drained, rich potting mix. Keep well watered.

Sagina glabra
(Pearlwort)
Mat-forming perennial that looks similar to moss, with tiny stems of white flowers in summer. Grow in sun or semishade in medium-rich potting mix. Use as underplanting for shrubs in containers.

Salvia
Sage
The frost-hardy herb, *S. officinalis*, and the half-hardy perennial, *S. splendens*, and its cultivars make good pot plants. Grow in sun in well-drained, medium-rich potting mix. Feed twice monthly during growing season.

Saxifraga
(Saxifrage)
Rosette-forming perennials. Mossy varieties have pale flowers on tall, thin stems in late spring, and grow in any well-drained soil in shade or semishade.

Scabiosa caucasica
(Scabious)
Perennial producing masses of pink flowers from early summer until autumn. Grow in sun or semishade in medium-rich potting mix. Deadhead regularly or, for attractive seedheads, allow flowers to go to seed.

Scaevola emula
(Scaevola)
Frost-tender, summer-flowering annual producing flowering spikes of lavender-blue flowers over long period of time. Grow in medium-rich potting mix in sunny site.

Tolmiea menziesii
(Piggyback Plant)
Just-hardy, evergreen perennial grown as houseplant. Baby plants grow on top of leaves. Plant in medium-rich potting mix in shady site. Water well in summer.

Tradescantia fluminensis
(Tradescantia; Wandering Jew)
Frost-tender, evergreen perennial grown for its ornamental foliage. Plant in shady or semishaded site in well-drained, medium-rich potting mix.

Vinca major
(Greater Periwinkle)
Hardy, evergreen perennials with trailing habit and blue or white flowers in spring and summer months. Grow in semishaded site in medium-rich potting mix.

Viola
(Pansy and Violet)
Low-growing perennial used as annual. Grow in semishade or sun in well-drained, rich potting mix. Water and feed with high-phosphorus liquid fertilizer during growing season.

Zantedeschia
(Calla Lily)
Frost-tender, tuberous perennials. *Z. aethiopica* has white spathes and *Z. rehmannii* has pink spathes in spring and summer. Grow in well-drained, rich potting mix, in semishade, in sheltered position.

Zebrina pendula
(Wandering Jew)
Similar to *Tradescantia fluminensis*, this tender, trailing perennial has purple and silver leaves. Grow in semishade in well-drained, medium-rich potting mix.

ANNUALS

Ageratum houstonianum
(Ageratum)
Annual with lilac-blue, pink, or white flowers. Plant in sun in well-drained, medium-rich potting mix. Feed weekly in summer and dead-head regularly.

Antirrhinum majus
(Snapdragon)
Perennial best grown as annual. Varieties available in red, pink, orange, yellow, and white. Plant in sun in well-drained, medium-rich potting mix. Feed weekly in flowering season. Water well.

Bellis perennis
(Double English Daisy)
Biennial usually grown as annual. Produces large numbers of double daisy flowers in spring and early summer in white, red, and pink. Plant in well-drained, medium-rich potting mix, and grow in sun or semishade. Deadhead blooms regularly to increase number of flowers produced.

Brachycome iberidifolia
(Swan River Daisy)
Hardy, bushy annual with green leaves and blue, lilac, or pink daisylike flowers in summer and early autumn. Plant in sun or semishade in medium-rich potting mix. Feed weekly.

Coleus blumei
(Coleus)
Frost-tender, bushy, evergreen perennial grown as annual for its ornamental, brightly colored leaves. Plant in well-drained, medium-rich potting mix in bright shade. Feed twice monthly. Remove flower spikes as they appear for best leaf color.

Cosmos 'Sunny Gold'
Bushy annual with feathery leaves and large golden flowerheads in summer and early autumn. Plant in sun in well-drained, medium-rich potting mix.

Delphinium consolida
(Larkspur)
Summer-flowering annual with spires of flowers in true blue, pink, and white. Plant in sun in well-drained, medium-rich potting mix. Feed once a week.

Diascia
Slightly tender perennials grown as annuals, producing succession of pink flowers through summer and autumn. Grow in well-drained, medium-rich potting mix in sun or semishade. Good for hanging baskets and wall baskets.

Eustoma grandiflorum
(Prairie Gentian)
Annual with gray-green leaves, producing succession of pink, blue, and pure white blooms during summer months. Grow in well-drained, rich potting mix in sunny site, and feed weekly.

Impatiens
(Impatiens)
Frost-tender annuals producing wealth of red, pink, orange, and white single and double blooms from late spring until first frosts. Grow in sun, semishade, or shade in well-drained medium-rich potting mix and keep well watered. Feed weekly.

Lobelia erinus
(Lobelia)
Summer-flowering annual, either trailing or low mounding. True blue as well as pink, lilac, and white varieties available; good for filling out windowboxes, hanging baskets, sinks, and troughs.

Lotus berthelotii
(Lotus)
Frost-tender, trailing perennial usually grown as annual. Produces scarlet flowers in good summers, but worth growing just for its silver-green foliage. Plant in medium-rich potting mix in sun. Water well in growing season.

Monopsis lutea
(Lutea)
Frost-tender, evergreen trailing perennial grown as annual with small green leaves and yellow flowers. Plant in sun in well-drained, medium-rich potting mix and feed weekly.

Ocimum basilicum
(Basil)
Frost-tender perennial grown as annual. Grow in sun in medium-rich potting mix. Several varieties available with good flavor and attractive leaf color.

Pelargonium
(Geranium)
Frost-tender, evergreen perennials mostly grown as annuals. Flowers in reds, purples, pinks, oranges, and white. Available as trailing (ivy-leaved) and upright (zonal) varieties and those with sweet-scented foliage. Grow in sun or semishade in medium-rich potting mix. Water well in flowering season. Feed weekly.

Petroselinum crispum
(Parsley)
Biennial best grown as annual. Plant in sun or semishade in well-drained, rich potting mix.

Petunia x hybrida
(Petunia)
Perennials grown as summer-flowering annuals with large trumpet-shaped flowers in white, yellow, red, pink, lilac, and purple. Grow in medium-rich potting mix in sun. Feed weekly.

Phacelia campanularia
(Phacelia)
Moderately fast-growing, hardy bushy annual with intense true blue bell-shaped flowers in summer and autumn. Grow in sun in rich potting mix.

Phlox
Low-growing species, such as *P. drummondii*, have pink, white, red, blue, purple, and lilac flowers in summer, and are well suited to pot culture. Plant in well-drained, medium-rich potting mix in sun or semishade. Feed once a week with high phosphorus fertilizer.

Reinwardtia trigyna
(Reinwardtia)
Frost-tender, low-growing annual with white flowers in summer. Grow in sun or semishade in medium-rich potting mix. Water well during growing season; good for hanging basket displays.

Tagetes
(Marigold)
Annuals such as *T. erecta* and *T. patula* have orange flowers in summer and autumn. Grow in sun in medium-rich potting mix.

Tropaeolum majus
(Nasturtium)
Fast-growing, bushy annual with red, orange, or yellow flowers for several months. Grow in sun in well-drained potting mix. Dead-head regularly for best results.

Verbena x hybrida
(Verbena)
Summer-flowering perennial grown as annual with clusters of flowers in red, pink, apricot, and white. Grow in sun in medium-rich potting mix. Water well in summer and feed weekly.

BULBS, CORMS, AND TUBERS

Allium schoenoprasum
(Chives)
Clump-forming, spring-flowering bulb with narrow, erect, dark green leaves used for cooking. Grow in sunny location in well-drained, medium-rich potting mix.

Clivia miniata
(Clivia)
Frost-tender, rhizomatous perennial with decorative, straplike leaves and heads of trumpet-shaped orange flowers. Grow in semishade in well-drained, medium-rich potting mix. Leave plant in same container for several years where it will thrive since it enjoys being pot-bound.

Crocus
(Crocus)
Frost-hardy, spring-flowering species for growing in containers. Choose from range of colored varieties. Plant in medium-rich potting mix in sun or semishade.

Cyclamen
Hardy to frost-tender tubers producing flowers in autumn, winter, or spring, in red, pink, and white. *C. coum*, *C. cyprium* and *C. hederifolium* are hardy. *C. persicum* produces tender florists' varieties.

Dahlia
Frost-tender, tuberous perennials producing single and double flowers in vibrant and pastel colors. Plant in sun in medium-rich potting mix. Water freely and feed once a week.

Fritillaria meleagris
(Snake's-head Fritillary)
Spring-flowering bulbs with bell-shaped flowers distinguished by snakeskin markings. Plant in sun or semishade in well-drained, medium-rich potting mix, and after flowering plant out into grass to naturalize in garden.

Hyacinthus
(Hyacinth)
Frost-hardy, spring-flowering bulbs, mostly scented; ideal for pot culture both indoors and outdoors. Grow in sun or semishade in well-drained, medium-rich potting mix.

Iris reticulata
(Reticulata Iris)
Spring-flowering miniature iris with sweet scent. Plant bulbs in sun or semishade. Grow in well-drained, medium-rich potting mix and keep just moist during winter.

Lilium
(Lily)
Mainly summer-flowering bulbs, many with scented, trumpet-shaped blooms in variety of colors. Grow in sun or semishade in rich potting mix. Water well and feed once a week with high-phosphorus liquid fertilizer.

Muscari
(Grape Hyacinth)
Spring-flowering bulbs with scented blue spires of flowers. Grow in well-drained, medium-rich potting mix in sunny site. Keep just moist through winter, but withhold water if freezing.

Narcissus
(Daffodil)
Spring-flowering bulbs. Popular cultivars such as 'Paperwhite' and 'Soleil d'Or' are ideal for indoor displays. For outdoor displays choose sweetly scented narcissus, such as *N.* 'Trevithian', *N.* 'Silver Chimes', *N. jonquilla*, and *N. poeticus*. Plant in sun or semishady site in well-drained, medium-rich potting mix.

Scilla
Spring-flowering bulbs with blue or white flowers. Plant bulbs in autumn and grow in sun or semishade in well-drained medium-rich potting mix.

Tulipa
(Tulip)
Spring-flowering bulbs available in many colors. Grow in sun or semishade in medium-rich potting mix. Plant in autumn. Keep soil just moist throughout winter, but withhold water if temperature falls below freezing.

CACTI AND OTHER SUCCULENTS

Crassula lycopodioides
(Crassula)
Frost-tender, pale gray-stemmed succulent with insignificant leaves. Grow indoors in bright site, in well-drained, medium-rich potting mix with equal quantity of coarse sand added. Water sparingly.

Echeveria harmsii
(Echeveria)
Frost-tender, silver-leaved succulent usually grown as houseplant. Thrives outdoors in summer if located in sunny sheltered site. Plant in gritty potting mix and water sparingly.

Gasteria verrucosa
(Gasteria)
Frost-tender succulent with fleshy, green, white-spotted leaves. Grow in bright site in well-drained, medium-rich potting mix with grit added. Keep planting fairly dry during winter.

Haworthia attenuata
(Haworthia)
Frost-tender, fleshy succulent with triangular, smooth green leaves with attractive silver markings. Grow in bright shade in well-drained, medium-rich potting mix.

Kalanchoe
Frost-tender, evergreen succulents with fleshy leaves and showy red, pink, and yellow flowerheads in spring. *K. pumila* has silver velvety leaves and lilac-pink flowers in spring. Excellent as indoor plants.

Nopalxochia phyllanthoides
(Orchid Cactus)
Frost-tender, perennial cactus with flattish stems producing lily-shaped pink flowers in spring. Grow indoors in warm, light situation in rich potting mix. Feed twice monthly in late summer and autumn. Keep just moist in winter.

Sedum
(Stonecrop)
Evergreen succulents with pink and yellow flowers, mostly in summer and autumn. Many, such as *S. acre* and *S. spathulifolium*, grow well in alpine troughs. Plant in sun in medium-rich potting mix.

Sempervivum
(Hens and Chicks)
Rosette-forming, evergreen perennials grown for their fleshy leaves. Grow outdoors in sun, in sheltered position, and plant in well-drained, gritty, low-nutrient potting mix.

Senecio
Large genus of plants including frost-tender succulents *S. articulatus* and *S. kleinii*, with gray-blue stems and smooth, glossy leaves. Grow indoors in well-drained, medium-rich potting mix with grit added to aid drainage. (*See also Trees and Shrubs.*)

Tender (frost-tender): severely damaged or killed by frost
Half-hardy: withstands light frost
Hardy (frost-hardy): not damaged by frost, but deeper cold may be lethal.

INDEX

ACKNOWLEDGMENTS

Author's Acknowledgments

Foremost thanks to my business partner Quentin Roake who, with his perceptive thoughts and great enthusiasm and energy, has shared in the creation of this book.

To photographer Matthew Ward for his splendid studio and location pictures and for always making all the work seem so easy.

To Bella Pringle and Louise Bruce, project editor and art editor, who, with their expertise and commitment, made this book on container gardening such fun to produce.

To Nick Lawrence of Landscape Management Construction for providing us with growing space and for watering the plantings.

To William Broadbent, Clifton Nurseries Ltd., May Cristea, Mrs. Franklin and Sarah Franklin, Fiona Hervey, Pauline and Richard Lay, Jenny and Richard Raworth, and Mrs. Reiss-Edwards, for allowing us to photograph our container plantings in their gardens.

Photographer's Acknowledgments

Steven Wooster, our additional location photographer, would also like to thank the following garden owners and designers for allowing their gardens and conservatories to be photographed for this book:
Beth Chatto, Mr. and Mrs. N. Coote, Mrs. Forrest, Mr. and Mrs. A. Huntington, Mr. and Mrs. J. Hilton, Mrs. Ingram/Maria Dallow (Flowers Galore), Mr. and Mrs. Hugh Johnson, Prue and Martin Lane-Fox, Major and Mrs. Mordaunt-Hare, Mr. and Mrs. C. Newman, Anthony Noel, Mr. and Mrs. Paice, Anthony Paul, Jenny and Richard Raworth, and Martin Summers.

Publisher's Acknowledgments

Dorling Kindersley would also like to thank Alan Hemsley for invaluable help with plant identification; Super Scenes for painting the background for each season opener; Vanessa Luff and Debbie Myatt for illustrations; Irene Lyford for editorial help; Lesley Riley for proofreading; Michael Allaby for the index.

Picture Credits

All photographs in this book were taken by Matthew Ward, with the exception of the following, listed below:
Peter Anderson 146b; 148b; 151t; 152b; 153b. **Lynne Brotchie (Garden Picture Library)** 8; 14br; 45t. **Jonathan Buckley** 98t; 138. **Brian Carter (Garden Picture Library)** 20. **John Glover (Garden Picture Library)** 16b; 18l. **Stephen Hayward** 9; 17bl; 26; 46; 52-53; 61; 64; 67; 73; 75; 94; 100; 116; 120; 130; 144. **Roger Hyam (Garden Picture Library)** 44; 45. **Diana Miller** 39; 40; 42; 51; 122tr. **Clive Nichols** 12t (The Old Rectory, Sudborough, Northants); 16t (The National Asthma Campaign Garden, Chelsea Flower Show 1993); 17t (The Old School House, Castle Hedingham) 77br (The Old Rectory, Sudborough, Northants); 84b (Butterstream, County Meath, Ireland. Designer: Jim Reynolds); 91t (17, Fulham Park Gardens, London. Designer: Anthony Noel); 105br (The Old School House, Castle Hedingham). **Gary Rogers (Garden Picture Library)** 25; 105t. **David Russell (Garden Picture Library)** 45br. **Ron Sutherland (Garden Picture Library)** 70b. **Juliette Wade (Garden Picture Library)** 15b; 18r. **Steven Wooster** 12b; 13tl; 13tr; 22t; 22b; 24; 38; 58t; 65t; 65br; 70; 77t; 77bl; 98b; 104; 122tl; 139.